AN EXECUTIVE'S COMPLETE GUIDE TO LICENSING

AN EXECUTIVE'S COMPLETE GUIDE TO LICENSING

Roger A. McCaffrey
and
Thomas A. Meyer

Dow Jones-Irwin
Homewood, Illinois 60430

This publication is designed to provide accurate and authoritative information in regard to the subject matter covered. It is sold with the understanding that neither the author nor the publisher is engaged in rendering legal, accounting, or other professional service. If legal advice or other expert assistance is required, the services of a competent professional person should be sought.

From a Declaration of Principles jointly adopted by a Committee of the American Bar Association and a Committee of Publishers.

Sponsoring editor: Susan Glinert Stevens, Ph.D.
Project editor: Susan Trentacosti
Production manager: Ann Cassady
Cover designer: Michael Finkleman
Compositor: TCSystems, Inc.
Typeface: 11/13 Times Roman
Printer: The Maple-Vail Book Manufacturing Group

Library of Congress Cataloging-in-Publication Data

McCaffrey, Roger A.
    An executive's complete guide to licensing / Roger A. McCaffrey
and Thomas A. Meyer.
        p.   cm.
    Includes index.
    ISBN 1-55623-134-2
    1. License agreements—United States.   2. Merchandise licensing—
—United States.   I. Meyer, Thomas A.   II. Title.
KF3145.M37   1989
343.73′07—dc19
[347.3037]   89–1118
                                                                    CIP

Printed in the United States of America

1 2 3 4 5 6 7 8 9 0 MP 6 5 4 3 2 1 0 9

For Miriam and Priscilla

ACKNOWLEDGMENTS

The following friends or associates read parts of our manuscript and in some cases contributed suggestions to improve it: Harry Weber, Dave Gosnell and Bob Silver of Conposit, Inc., and Tom Sullivan. Maureen McCaffrey and Neil McCaffrey helped in the early stages, before Dow Jones-Irwin signed us. Special thanks to Ernie Lustenring of *The Licensing Book* for his help in lining up just the right photos to use. Tom Meyer also wishes to thank Art Gramer and Richard Waters for their help in the first phase of Meyer Management's existence.

Roger A. McCaffrey
Thomas A. Meyer

CONTENTS

AN EXECUTIVE'S COMPLETE GUIDE TO LICENSING

INTRODUCTION

Before this book was written, other titles on licensing were researched and not a single one was found to provide an all-encompassing look at the guiding theories of the practice. Perhaps $75 billion (no one really knows exactly) is generated annually by licensing. Yet, aside from technical legal treatments and a get-rich-quick paperback on the subject, no other books have been written about it.

It speaks volumes that so little is known of a field that is growing by leaps and bounds. It says that there are too few people with a complete grasp of what could someday be a nearly trillion dollar "industry." Actually, licensing isn't really an industry, any more than "food" is. Licensing is a skill; part art and part science. It can be applied to diverse businesses—almost any kind, any size. It is this book's job to show you how licensing works, providing the theory and concrete examples. It will be your job to apply the principles to your particular industry and company, or to your property or product idea. We trust that once you have read this book, you will find you can handle that challenge.

Our experience in licensing dates back several years, when one of us was given the opportunity to help Anheuser-Busch build its licensing program, a program that became the envy of many in corporate America, and in a sense helped show the way for big licensors like The Coca-Cola Company. There were numerous contacts with people thinking about starting licensing programs, and many of them got into licensing (as licensors) in the wrong way: Licensees or someone in the licensor's own company would approach them with a good product idea; the licensor would deliberate and then go ahead with the licensed product—and it might have succeeded. But that isn't the way to build a licensing program. In fact, one of the central themes of this book is that a single product success does not a licensing program make.

Presented here are the correct theory and rationale for a licensor's becoming involved in licensing. And you will find a plan for a full licensing program, both for the individual with a bright idea and for the corporate executive. In the process this book will also instruct licensees in the licensing skill as well; but note that as a rule, it is addressed to licensors, since they generally steer licensing programs. Usually the licensor draws up the contract or has the final say, even when the licensee provides the product concept.

In addressing the licensor unless otherwise explicitly stated, we don't slight the licensee. While it suffices for the licensor to know a defined set of things (detailed herein) about the licensee, the licensee must know as much as possible about the overall licensing plan of his licensor partner. Any licensee reading this book, we predict, will not miss a page. The more a licensee knows about the components of a good licensing program, the more successful his or her licensing agreements can be.

Many people categorize licensing into groups such as sports licensing, or lifestyle licensing, or character, entertainment, design or fashion, or corporate licensing. All such terms, useful as far as they go, tend to obfuscate the real nature of licensing, and can almost by themselves dissuade someone from getting into licensing. If the property doesn't fit into any of the above categories, many might doubt that they have a license-able property. Wrong. Almost anything can be licensed—not just trademarks or brands, company names and technology, but also graphic designs, products privately developed, or new properties with absolutely no track record. This book groups licensing into three broad categories (see the Glossary and Chapter 1) which encompass all the properties just listed.

So not all licensing fits the commonly used categories, and, of course, not all licensing is "brand extension." It certainly is *property* extension, however. Even though not all licensing is brand extension, for the purposes of this book we address the typical licensor—a company with a brand/trademark it wants to extend into other product categories via licensing. This way, all bases are covered. Brand extension licensing for a consumer products company demands the most complete description of the practice. Those involved in different licensing can easily factor out anything said that doesn't apply to them.

For instance, if you're a graphic artist who has developed a great cartoon character, you don't want brand extension—but you do want "brand expansion." Most of the points made about brand extension also apply to brand expansion.

Before diving into the depths, let us take you through the same exercise that we take a typical potential licensor through when invited to discuss brand extension/licensing possibilities. The most frequently asked questions about licensing are listed—with short answers. By the time you've read the book, every point will be elaborated upon, but what follows will give you an overview of the chapters:

Question 1: What are the major risks in licensing?

First, understand that there are *perceived* risks by apprehensive potential licensors, and there are real risks. The perceived risk: many fear they will lose control of the property, particularly a trademark. Others fear the whole licensing operation will go out of control. Neither has to happen. The real risk: undertaking a licensing effort without a comprehensive plan or a proper understanding of how licensing works and what benefits it brings. It's *not* just a promotional vehicle or an income producer, for example.

Question 2: Won't there be an added administrative burden? Can that be reduced?

Yes, extra time will be spent by some executives if the program is well run. But you can save time by researching the industries you are thinking about entering, narrowing down your contacts to the best possible licensees, meeting them in a methodical way, using a standardized contract that can be adapted to each licensee, and carefully selecting the product categories you wish to enter.

Question 3: What are the principal responsibilities of the licensor? Do we have to guarantee the licensee's inventory?

No, you don't. As for the responsibilities, you should support and use the licensee whenever possible. Keep the licensee updated on new marketing developments in your industry and in your company. Do such things as bringing the licensee into any promotional programs you can.

Question 4: Can we control the licensee's distribution avenues?

Yes, the contract can specify the kind of distribution you want the licensee to sell in.

Question 5: Do we have to give the licensee an exclusive?

It's not a must, but it's a good practice, and good licensees expect it (in most product categories). It's also an incentive to the licensee to be more productive.

Question 6: Do we have to have one royalty rate for all our licensees, no matter what the product?

No, it depends on the product category, because the profit margins and volume will vary with the product.

Question 7: What are the most important ingredients in a licensor–licensee relationship?

Be forthright, and make sure before you start that each fulfills a need for the other.

Question 8: What are the characteristics of a good licensee?

A solid management team, including deep enough talent in that area; resourcefulness; and sound financing.

Question 9: How long does it take to develop a relationship with a licensee?

Between three months and a year. A year if the project is complex, as is the case in "business-to-business" licensing. If you take more than a year, something is probably wrong with your effort, or with the licensee's.

Question 10: What's our financial commitment likely to be?

Minimal. Your major start-up costs will be: (1) hiring talent or developing it internally, (2) some travel for trade shows and licensee contacts, (3) legal costs associated with development of a standard contract and any contract negotiating, and (4) cost of announcing the program in licensing and industry trade publications. Generally, within two years, your licensing program should be self-funding, and then some.

Question 11: In the beginning, how do we know if we have a property we can license?

Here are two good indicators of your potential: (1) You have a loyal consumer base, and (2) you've carved out a unique position in your market.

Question 12: What's the timetable for profitability?

At the two-year mark, you should be profitable, and the program should stay that way. You *could* be in the black as early as the 12- to 18-month mark, depending on how much strategic planning you've done before searching for licensees, and on how fast you recruit the licensees you want.

Question 13: Should the licensor look into more than one industry category at a time?

Yes, look into as many as possible without overburdening your licensing people.

Question 14: Does licensing increase—or decrease—the strength of our trademark?

In a good program, increase. In a poorly run program (where haphazard practices and carelessness reign), decrease.

Question 15: What's a popular reason other companies get into licensing?

Two good reasons, in this order: income potential and exposure.

Question 16: What are the most important factors for a solid licensing program?

The concepts should be original. Coke apparel bested Pepsi because Coke got there first, and Pepsi copied the leader. Secondary (but important) factors in a solid licensing program: sound management and good business judgment.

Question 17: Should we test licensing the way we would a new product?

No, because licensing isn't like a new product. It's a new business *tool* with broader implications than a new product. If *one* licensed product fails a marketing test, it doesn't follow that you should call off the entire licensing program, but if a new product entry flunks *its* test, obviously you pull it back.

Question 18: Hasn't licensing peaked?

No, although there seems to be a glut of mediocre products. There is never a glut of good ones, however. There was a shakeout in the "industry" recently, and some people lost money, tempted by exaggerated claims about huge profit potential.

CHAPTER 1

WHAT IS LICENSING?

If your company were to receive a gift of 10,000 acres of Alaskan oil fields, you'd view it in much the same way we urge you to see a licensing program: uncharted, but with tremendous potential. Nothing may come of your decision to explore licensing, and you may have good reasons not to follow through with a program. But to view licensing as anything less than a major new source of income, or at least advertising and promotion, would be a mistake. The first task in Chapter 1 is to show how the licensor, as distinct from the licensee, should approach a licensing effort. There are three major kinds of licensing, and they are defined in this chapter. Then you will look at licensing from a licensee's perspective and see what the licensee should expect in a licensing arrangement.

In the second half of this chapter, you will be looking at your company and its future in a fresh way and see why, to succeed in licensing over the long term, you must expand your company's horizons. This isn't to suggest that you radically restructure your company. At the end of the chapter we'll explain the proper corporate view of the licensing program you undertake and list who in the company should understand licensing (and why). Finally, we'll debunk a few myths about licensing that are even now, despite all the licensing success stories in circulation, believed by many.

THE LICENSOR AND THE LICENSOR'S PERSPECTIVE

Promotional Licensing

Licensing can be used simply as a vehicle by which to extend your company's merchandising efforts. In the area of sales promotion, a fictional example would be *Star Wars* trading cards offered in a box of

6

• People call it "lifestyle" licensing, but that's really another variation of "promotional licensing." (Courtesy the Nancy Bailey Company, Edelson & Sons the licensee.)

General Mills breakfast cereal. In the broader field of sales *and* advertising, a company such as Anheuser-Busch gives its brand name to other companies (i.e., to licensees, who will use the name on items as diverse as T-shirts and collector tins or ceramic plates).

New Product Development Licensing

This is a more sophisticated form in which a licensee will use someone else's name, company logo or image, brand, character, or whatever part of a property deemed suitable, for a major new product entry. The licensor benefits because a new business opportunity is provided, possibly giving him entry into an industry otherwise beyond reach. The Sporting News® Baseball™ computer game, a licensing deal with EPYX, a computer game software company, fits this description. The licensee, a medium-sized company, obviously benefits by expanding its market manyfold. Moreover, the licensee is worth every penny it makes from the arrangement because it provides the licensor expertise to succeed in a new business.

• Promotional licensing differs markedly from new product development licensing or business-to-business licensing. Products licensed by Burger King, 7UP, and Coke for promotional purposes appear here. (Courtesy Nancy Bailey & Associates, Inc., and The Coca-Cola Company, respectively.)

Business-to-Business (or Service-to-Service) Licensing

This involves the naming of a company or division with the brand name or corporate name of some other property. For example, Wilson Sporting Goods joined with Sports Apparel Corporation, which formed the Wilson Apparel Division, a multimillion dollar clothing company, for the sole purpose of manufacturing and marketing apparel under the Wilson brand name. Popeye's Restaurants is another example, fitting perfectly into the service-to-service category. The J. G. Hook/Disney partnership is a third example. Their "Mickey and Company" was a retail store chain. Admittedly, the risks and stakes begin to rise when business-to-business licensing is introduced, because you've erected a whole new company. But with proper management at the top of the licensing program, business-to-business licensing can work well.

A good licensing program should afford your company the opportunity to work within all three main licensing categories. One way to ensure that that *won't* happen, one way to ensure that your licensing program operates poorly, is to put a licensing program under a second-

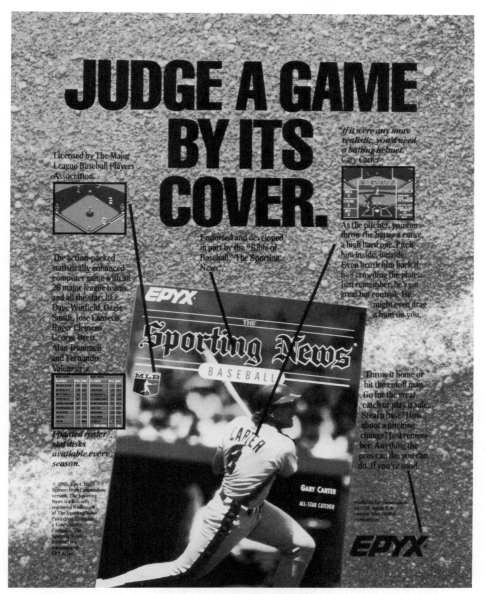

• The Sporting News® Baseball™ computer game demonstrates the use of a licensed name to increase credibility of a lesser-known (to sports fans) licensee. (©EPYX, Inc.)

ary marketing position in the company, such as merchandising or sales promotion. In these divisions a licensing effort is hidden from the top people in the corporation, and they won't be able to make the day-to-day decisions about some of their company's most valuable assets.

The central element to almost any licensing effort is the brand name, company name, or logo. Top management should continuously monitor how they are being used and what kind of business people and businesses are associating with the corporate name. Unlike the stock market, where the higher the risk the higher the potential return, in licensing, the higher the risk the *lower* the return, because you're risking your company's reputation.

But that hasn't stopped some companies from making careless mistakes, usually due to misconceptions. One such misconception, not quite as common as it used to be (particularly in the beverage industry), is that if you can get free exposure by licensing your logo or brand name, you should do it. Free exposure was then compensation enough. Licensors are generally smarter than that these days. Especially for the beginner it's important to point out that offering your name to someone cheaply and with low profit expectations does not guarantee a flood of proposals from potential licensees. If anything, the opposite can occur. If you treat your valuable trademark *as such,* you'll attract better-quality licensees, who will respect you and your demands, including a fair price. This is precisely what happened to a big licensor in the early

• **The Doughboy™: a "plush toy" promotional licensing item. For years he was squeezed or poked on TV by housewives, and now kids can do it. A clever use of licensing, bringing a commercial character into consumer homes.** (Courtesy the Nancy Bailey Company.)

1980s. The more standards this licensor instituted and the higher the royalty demands (way too low originally), the more licensees came knocking. No licensee *thanked* anybody for the higher figure, mind you. Some complained, but the licensor explained that the trademark was worth the 7 percent of wholesale price on any item, for after all, it was primarily purchased because of the logo on it. (The royalty required had been as low as 3 percent of wholesale price.)

The potential licensor must note that, whatever opportunities there are in the area of promotional licensing, it is new product development licensing and business-to-business licensing where there is real ground to be broken. Consequently, *licensing should have the attention of the senior management*—and some of the *brightest and most imaginative people* working under them. Harnessing their talents is the job of a top executive who knows new product or new business development, marketing, and the financial end (to evaluate licensees); and any legal experience is helpful.

THE LICENSEE AND THE LICENSEE'S PERSPECTIVE

Much more often than not, the licensee is an unknown company (at least to the consumer) that is given immediate access to a heretofore undreamt-of consumer base loyal to the licensor. Though this is by no means always the case, we'll address the small licensee in this section. Licensing is at once a benefit and a challenge for the licensee. Will the partnership work?

The licensee may well be a smallish company thrust into partnership with a corporation having its own "corporate culture," to use a popular phrase. Before signing any contract, the licensee should be thoroughly familiar with the licensor and how it does business and deals with outside people. Is there a sizable corporate bureaucracy you'll encounter? Exactly who from the licensor will make the decisions that will affect a major part of your business? The licensee should expect clear answers to such questions—and the licensor should provide them. Neither partner should proceed if there are any ambiguities or doubts about them.

If the licensee can find someone within its ranks who has been part of a larger corporation, he or she may help colleagues to realize that corporations don't run the way small companies do. Almost every licensee, for example, expects decisions from bigger licensors in a matter of weeks. Most corporations take *months*.

Another crucial question for the licensee is: How will the licensor view and manage the licensing program? If it's a central operation in a corporation, if it has a "priority" rating, then a licensee can usually expect to be treated with respect and appreciation. But if the licensor tends to view the effort as a get-rich-quick endeavor, or for that matter a secondary marketing function with senior management uninvolved, then the licensee should be wary. It's doubtful he'll benefit in the long run.

The licensee should also take a long look at the potential licensor's business. What is the distribution system like? Do you see any weaknesses in sales and marketing? What does the corporation's balance sheet look like? You might even check into their accounting firm. Moreover, on the positive side of the ledger, a close inspection of the licensor's business(es) can give the licensee a better idea of the *benefits* he can provide to the licensor.

The licensee should expect long-term commitment and support of the licensed property. This doesn't always apply (it wouldn't, say, in the case of a World Champion sports team or a Player of the Year, or for a movie-related product). But in trademark licensing and most other forms, the licensee should expect answers to questions like these:

1. What are the promotional plans for the product over the next couple of years? What is the advertising budget?
2. What kind of multiple sales support efforts will the licensor put behind the product?
3. What is the brand's life cycle? At what stage is it? Is it growing? When does the licensor plan to phase it out?
4. Are there other licensees? How are they promoting the property? Are you expected to work in tandem with the other effort, and will that help you?

If the licensed product is a packaged consumer item like a cereal, bread, or a beverage, the licensee should expect some space (at some point; *not* permanently) on the package for advertising the licensed product. This will have to be negotiated with the licensor, of course, and carefully planned so as not to divert attention from the primary product itself. But it's safe to say that on most packaging, there's room for the licensee.

• Licensing tied to the film industry can be both risky and, in the case of movies like *Top Gun*, possibly lucrative. (Officially licensed merchandise from the movie *Top Gun*, ™ & ©Paramount Pictures Corp. All rights reserved. Exclusively licensed to Joy Insignia, Inc., Deerfield Beach, Florida.)

Other "painless" ways for the licensor to help include:

- Coupons for "cross promoting" (e.g., putting ice cream product offerings into cookie packages).
- TV and radio commercial "tie-ins" making the licensed item a key part of the sale.
- "Tag-ons" at the end of commercials or in a print ad.
- Public relations assistance, if the licensor is big enough to have a PR department.

There are two dangers for a licensee. One of them has to do with a specific contractual obligation, the other with plain human exuberance. Most licensing deals call for the licensee to pay a royalty advance—a nonrefundable guarantee against royalties, in fact. Many licensees agree to pay too much. Which is to say, they expect too much in the way of sales. And the licensor, particularly if it's a big company, is accustomed to big dollar sales figures and projections. We can only offer a truism: if an idea is good and the marketing strategy works, the royalties will come. Licensors and licensees both should be patient. Moreover, licensees not willing to take a big gamble should consider walking away from a licensor who seems to want too much of an advance. This especially holds for short-term propositions such as motion picture-

•Licensees come in all shapes and sizes. The BIC Corporation, for example, dwarfs some of its licensors in size—and even competes with the National Football League in name recognition. With their lighters, BIC offers NFL teams an item that has retail potential and can double as an advertising speciality—a "giveaway." (Courtesy the BIC Corporation.)

related items: *E.T.* sweatshirts, for example. The licensor may have higher hopes than it should, even if the movie did set box office records. The public is fickle; fads have a way of dying just when businesses attempt to capitalize on them.

The other danger for a licensee is that after entering into an agreement, he allows his company to become overly dependent on the bigger company (the licensor's) for a large portion of business. You can't help it if the licensed product "takes off." After all, a success brings with it a demand for time and resources. Still, the licensee should engage in a continuous search for opportunities to diversify.

For example, a smallish screen-printing company recently signed a licensing agreement with a major beverage company to sell T-shirts featuring its popular advertising mascot. The licensee's business exploded. Understandably aggressive, the licensee nonetheless upset the licensor by straying beyond its allotted selling territory. A legal battle followed the cancellation of the licensing contract, and the screen-printing company was hurt financially—not just because of the legal bills. They hadn't diversified.

Licensors sometimes demand exclusivity from licensees, requiring that the licensee not do business with other licensors in the same product category. But this requirement should by no means tie a licensee to just one trademark. With a good licensor under its belt, in fact, the licensee will find it has added credibility with potential licensors in other business categories. But beyond that, as a licensee develops its product for the retail trade, it greatly increases its chances of success *for all products* if it has a diversified set of trademarks to offer. Approaching, say, K mart with Anheuser-Busch, Coca-Cola, and Hershey's apparel connections is far better than with only one of the three.

The best rule of thumb for a licensee: no matter how solid your licensing agreement, always be in a position to absorb the shock of that big corporate client pulling out.

Licensing/Joint Venture Combinations

Sometimes licensees find themselves in a position to enter into business relationships that can't be called "pure" licensing, though they include elements of licensing. For example, Hershey's Chocolate Milk, wherein the licensee uses the Hershey brand name but also buys syrup from Hershey's. Another example is Oreo Ice Cream, in which the ice cream manufacturer uses the Oreo packaging and name, but also buys the cookies for the ice cream from Nabisco.

Not all licensees are small, nor are all licensors big. But a "midget" licensee should be ready to point out abilities it has that a licensor of greater size doesn't. In short, show how it can complement the licensor's efforts. The licensor should welcome such a list of abilities. But it's up to the licensee to draw one up, both to help the business relationship and for negotiating purposes.

Occasionally, by the way, it is the licensor who is small. A classic case is the father-and-son team, Ray and Cliff Galbraith. Son Cliff invented 32 dinosaur characters ("Rockasaurus," "New Yorkasaurus," "Shopasaurus," "Skateboardasaurus," and "Baseball-asaurus," to name a few). The Galbraiths ran a very small screen-printing shop until their characters took America by storm. They're licensed to dozens of firms, and they're on everything from mugs to bed sheets. Macy's has featured the zany characters. Disney sells them. The

• **Super-talented artist Mary Engelbreit licenses some of her art to Sunrise Publications, Inc., for greeting cards. Her "Chair of Bowlies"© has also been licensed for dolls and figurines, among other things.** (Courtesy Mary Engelbreit.)

Galbraiths signed on a big licensee, Hallmark, early in the process, earning them credibility. But it was talent, not size, that made them winners.

LOOKING AT YOUR COMPANY AND ITS FUTURE IN NEW WAYS

Licensing requires you to look at your company in a fresh way. That will come naturally, in part. You'll have to reexamine, with an eye toward fitting in (or extracting, as the case may be) a licensed product, the following aspects in a disciplined manner: product name, advertising, distribution, promotion efforts, and most importantly, research/ development, where most new product concepts emanate.

All that will come automatically, but you'll also have to look beyond your core industry, since, by definition, licensing involves linking one business to another, unrelated enterprise. While that's also a natural process, what isn't so natural is the next step: thoroughly evaluating company "assets" or "equities" that are taken for granted. It could be something as obvious as a beautiful corporate logo you've taken for granted and never used to best advantage. It's usually lots of things in many different categories. A lot of companies take for granted a nontangible factor: the goodwill they've built among consumers.

During the evaluation period, when you take a new look at your company to determine what if any "equities" you have that will make a licensing program successful, you have an excellent time to discover something. You can find out how you are perceived by consumers. Even if you don't get into licensing, this evaluation is worthwhile. You can always learn from your customers. And you may also uncover a hidden liability you'll have to erase or turn into an asset.

There's another reason to take a hard look at your company. You may have a new product idea that a licensing deal can help you bring out cheaply. Indeed, licensing can provide a way to bypass a lot of the financial risk often associated with new product development, because not only are most expenses absorbed by a licensee, but you get the licensee's expertise at no cost. It is well to remember that the return on a licensing program is virtually all net income, in fact. While there may be administrative costs, there is certainly no "cost-of-goods-sold" figure—or a host of other marketing costs—that typically accompany a product or service.

How many new product ideas do you know about that were shelved for lack of funding or time? Could there have been a licensee willing to assume some of the risk for the new product? Quite possibly. More to the point, how many new products could your company generate if you had the benefit of a thorough evaluation session producing results like

• **Chuck Yeager and "Big Daddy" Don Garlits are two celebrities whose names are licensed to Revell, the model maker, which markets a line of "Yeager Superfighters" aircraft and the Don Garlits AA/FD Dragster.** (Courtesy Revell, Inc.)

those found in Appendix B, in the Licensing Evaluation Report written for an actual company (fictional name)?

A good licensing evaluation effort can all but transform a company. One pet food concern is a case in point. It's too early to say they've been wildly successful, but here's their story, in short form. They've been highly successful at selling their product, and partly as a result they haven't felt the need to break into a couple of expanding areas. One area is pet supplies; the other shall remain nameless, as the matter is delicate with some in the company. In any case, consultants at Conposit took this licensor through the evaluation stages. It was a revelation to them. They discovered that in the pet supply area, their name comes up as the people to buy from more often than their competitors'. The fact that they lack the expertise in most facets of the pet supply business doesn't matter—that's for their licensee to handle. And in the unmentionable area, the pet food client has decided to take a new look at the category they got burned in 15 years ago. The reason? This time, *they* won't have to cope with problems they encountered in the 1970s. Their licensee will—and will be only too happy to do so, since the licensor is a big name in the industry.

All companies continuously look to the future with one eye on the competition. Unfortunately, many companies perceive licensing as a distraction to their primary goal: making profits in their core business. But the fact is, licensing can help you expand—inexpensively—while at the same time enabling you to remain focused on the profit-generating staples. If your company enjoys a good reputation and/or has a recognizable trademark, you're probably underusing those equities if you're not licensing.

THE PROPER CORPORATE VIEW

While a licensee generally does the lion's share of the development, distribution, and merchandising, and indeed assumes the financial risk, it is nonetheless imperative that the licensor put together a quality licensing team of its own. After all, it is the licensor's family jewels that will be put in the display case; the good name of the company is priceless.

And beyond that important consideration, it's also vital to see that licensing is an integral part of whatever company is employing the tool.

It's "interdisciplinary," involving all these skills: legal, accounting, marketing, research, and new product development. Once this is understood, it is only reasonable to insist that your licensing manager be someone with a broad business background who answers directly to the chief executive officer. His department should be independent of all others, though it could work well as an adjunct of marketing or planning or business diversification departments. In Chapter 4 we'll explore more precisely what it takes to develop a crack licensing team.

WHO SHOULD UNDERSTAND LICENSING

Several kinds of corporate people, and some outside the corporate structure, would do well to know more about licensing. They are listed here, in no particular order. Why they should acquaint themselves with licensing is also briefly told.

Merger and Acquisition Specialists / "Corporate Raiders"

For these people, it's important that they find ways to get the most out of a company with the least amount of capital. Licensing is made to order, then, for many a corporation. Scaling a company down to size and squeezing all there is to squeeze out of every facet of the business is an approach compatible with the "licensing mentality," covered in Chapter 2.

It's appalling, though, how few corporate takeovers or mergers have resulted in a serious licensing effort by the new management. The only one that comes immediately to mind is William Stiritz at Ralston Purina Company. When they acquired Continental Baking, they realized they'd purchased not only some fine brands such as Hostess Twinkies and Wonder Bread, but wholesome reputations along with the trademarks. They set out to make the most of this equity, hiring licensing consultants (Conposit) to uncover dozens of possibilities for new products, all of which were to be designed to generate revenue *and* to support the core business.

Chief Executives

We've made it clear why company leaders should know about licensing. There's an understandable reason why they haven't known much until fairly recently. If top executives were at all familiar with licensing, they tended to know only bits and pieces, seeing the fruits of a program but thinking that their company wasn't right for such an undertaking. Licensing tended to be viewed as strictly in the domain of sports, entertainment, clothing design, and businesses of that nature. The central reason for executive misperceptions is simple: licensing is a new field. No business schools teach it. Few specialists were around to impart the knowledge to corporations. This book, in fact, is the first general theoretical treatment of the subject, even though licensing generates scores of billions in sales volume annually. Small wonder that chief executives, and most others in the business world, were slow to see the opportunities licensing afforded them.

Marketing Executives

Licensing know-how should be basic equipment for anyone involved on any level with product selling. Product or brand managers and their people center their lives around increasing their brand's sales. Along the way, they'll entertain every new promotion idea on the face of the earth, sometimes failing to recognize gold nuggets they've been sitting on.

Many people view licensing as something for the legal department; or as a gimmicky way to make the trademark more visible. This is a tendency found among marketing people as well.

Corporate or Business Lawyers

Some lawyers think of licensing as essentially legal in character. If they can write a licensing contract they feel they've understood this new dimension to business. But contracts are only part of the picture; and even here, the best of lawyers will consult closely with other arms of the licensing department. A lawyer conversant in licensing renders the most useful service when "translating" legalese for his licensing people's benefit—and rephrasing business terms into precise legal definitions.

Inventors, Graphic Artists

These people who create should at least be familiar with licensing. And we don't mean that they should just read *Advertising Age*. They'll certainly see the fruits of successful licensing there, but we're suggesting that they know licensing well enough to capitalize on their creations and to protect themselves.

• Those Characters From Cleveland, Inc., is a division of American Greetings Corporation, organized for the sole purpose of licensing. This was an adroit move on the part of American Greetings, normally the kind of company that would be a licensee for someone with a recognizable property. Above are four of "those characters." Strawberry Shortcake, not pictured here, is their best known. (Courtesy Those Characters From Cleveland, Inc./American Greetings Corporation.)

An actual example: an inventor of a revolutionary air cleansing product received a patent for it and approached an expert to help him market it on the large scale it deserved. The expert suggested he try licensing it to a major car company or retailer. (This would have been an arrangement similar to the Galbraiths' in that the *licensee* would have been the big corporate entity.) As usual, the expert explained that the inventor as licensor would get a royalty of 5 to 7½ percent of the wholesale price of his item. This wasn't enough for the inventor, and the project never got off the ground. It still hadn't—many years after the inventor first put out feelers.

Market Researchers

Countless millions are spent every year by major consumer products companies on market research to learn how their proposed new product or their present brand is operating. How do consumers perceive it? What kind of future response to the product can be expected? Important questions, indeed. But brand extension possibilities through licensing are routinely ignored in the research process. Even if a company never launched a brand extension/licensing effort, they would certainly have benefited, at little extra cost, from exploring the question in the traditional market research phase. If you look at the Conposit report in Appendix B, you'll note how easily this could have been worked into the typical market research analysis. And that's because licensing is partly *dependent* on market research.

Advertising People

Talented ad writers, we hold, would write even better copy and be more creative if they were introduced to the "licensing mentality." Not that advertising should be created for the sake of licensing, but a great ad campaign can actually provide the very basis of a licensing program. Efforts were made to talk the Gallo Company into making "Frank and Ed" of Bartles & Jaymes fame into licensed characters. Anheuser-Busch's "Spuds MacKenzie," created by a young account executive at DDB Needham, is a classic example of great advertising spawning great licensing. Granted, such programs tend to be short-lived, but they can provide, as in the case of Spuds, untold millions in free exposure.

Small Business Owners

Any small businessman with an idea should look into licensing as a way to develop the concept. We've seen what the Galbraiths did with dinosaurs. Another example is the Cabbage Patch Dolls, which were invented by an independent businessman who licensed them to Coleco Industries, Inc. The Pound Puppies' success story is similar to that of the Cabbage Patch Dolls.

New Product Developers

These professionals, like brand managers, have to be acquainted with all the needs of their company if they're to do the best possible job. One

• **Mom of the Year® was created by Colorworks, Ltd., and licensed by Alaska Momma, Inc., to CTI for balloons and to L. V. Myles for sleepwear. This a design tailor-made for licensing, as was the Galbraiths' (of Chapter 1).** (Courtesy Alaska Momma®, Inc.)

of the weapons they should have in their arsenal is licensing, because one of the key questions for any new product is, "How do we develop, expand and *keep* market share?" The Dole (as in fruit) people have shown the way in this regard. They took their equity and moved into products such as ice cream and frozen yogurt, enhancing sales of their primary product in the bargain. This is sometimes referred to as the "halo effect," and it is one that is more and more often employed by new product people.

MYTHS ABOUT LICENSING

There are lots of stubborn misperceptions about licensing, despite all lessons from the world of licensing to the contrary. This chapter will close with a list of the myths heard most often and a refutation of each one.

MYTH: Licensing your trademark will weaken your trademark.
Coca-Cola held that view for years. The opposite is closer to the truth, unless you do a poor job of licensing. Indeed, good licensing strengthens your trademark in other, secondary categories. Other corporations worry about losing control of their trademark, as distinct from weakening its promotional clout. But here again, it's more

accurate to say that good licensing provides an excellent way to exercise tighter *control* over your trademark. No, you don't need a battery of lawyers to do the job, as the book later explains.

MYTH: Licensing is wonderfully simple. Just give someone the use of your trademark and collect royalties.

Nothing could be further from the truth. While licensing isn't anything like starting a new company, it's still a function that requires a skilled professional team in the corporation.

MYTH: Licensing will divert attention from the primary company goals and take a great deal of time to administrate.

Half true. Licensing takes time and energy; you'll have to find the right administrator to lead the effort. But it shouldn't take a great deal of *time* from the corporate leaders. And compared to the potential net worth of the endeavor, it's the most efficient new project that your company can devote time to launching.

A good example: One of the authors of this book, after leaving a big corporate licensing program, spent two years in another division of the company, new product development. One product, among six or seven that he worked on, saw the light of day. It failed, as do the majority of new product efforts that start from scratch. Yet the company spent probably $50,000 *on his travel alone* in those two years. Had he spent that time in licensing, he thinks that he and his colleagues could easily have generated $50 million in sales and a few million in net profit. This doesn't include all the free advertising the company's products would have received through the licensing effort. Moreover, the whole department could have been staffed with no more than six full-time people.

MYTH: Licensing commits the licensor to ordering inventory that must be sold.

False, unless the licensor explicitly requests that. It is the licensee who must commit to inventory.

MYTH: Licensing puts a company or brand name at such risk that it is foolhardy to venture into any program.

There's a half truth here. An ill-conceived licensing program can indeed hurt a licensor's brand, and it could deal a blow to a licensee. But this is *not* to say that licensing is a gamble without predictable results. While no one knows how a product will fare until it's offered to consumers—in that sense, all of business is a risk—you *can* protect yourself with diligent planning and marketing. Even if your product isn't a winner, you'll by no means damage your company.

CHAPTER 2

THE "LICENSING MENTALITY"

Corporations tend to discourage original thinking. That's a central point of Tom Peters' runaway bestsellers, and it's become a cliche. But as Peters makes clear, it doesn't have to be that way, and the most successful or promising companies *encourage* new ideas. These companies stand the best chance of implementing and sustaining a licensing program.

Overly cautious thinking isn't found only in some big companies. The tendency to reject fresh approaches (or new product concepts) is a human one—and you'll find it in businesses of all sizes. So what follows isn't intended for big corporate people only. Moreover, this chapter only faintly echoes the aforementioned Peters theme. Because, while licensing requires original thinking, one thing it doesn't demand is a risk of capital on the part of licensors. Licensees incur that. Licensors' main concern should be protecting and enhancing the brand or company image.

To understand licensing, you must put yourself in a different frame of mind. You have to look *outside* your company's business parameters. You have to search for unused or wasted company "assets," intangibles like consumer loyalty to your brand or a strong company reputation. Lastly, you must think of ways to leverage these assets, these nonfinancial equities. Let's look at all three musts.

LOOKING OUTSIDE COMPANY PARAMETERS

If an executive at any level of your company were to spend his or her time looking at practically every industry to see if your company could compete in it, you'd normally wonder if the executive had lost all sense of direction. But licensing consultants are paid by potential licensors and licensees to do exactly that. Because there is little or no financial risk for licensors, they lose nothing by looking.

Licensors should be prepared to look at other industries with imagination and enthusiasm. Admittedly, most people who manage businesses seldom care to spend time beyond their own industry category. They find it enough to constantly readjust to their own market base and to their competition. But that's the *minimum* any company can do. When times get tough, is the minimum enough? When the boss grumbles about weak numbers, is the minimum from you enough?

Your title or job description should not prohibit your having innovative ideas for producing profits, any more than it should keep you from learning all the other facets of your company's business. And in fact, the licensing mentality depends in part on a solid grasp of the business you're in. Some of the best licensing people we've known are those who have had to run a business and not had the luxury of specializing in distribution or finance or some other category. They're "nuts and bolts" types. They have the big picture. They wouldn't strike you as remarkable in any particular way; they're certainly not known as experts in any one field. And they probably wouldn't strike you as creative. But they certainly can be. As you can, most likely.

"Creative" is one of the most used, but least understood, words in business life, in our opinion. If someone's in advertising, for example, he or she is dubbed creative almost automatically. Yet time and again, in both new product development and licensing, we've seen many of the best ideas come from the most unlikely sources. We can't be the only one to have witnessed this phenomenon, but we've seen average folks in focus group research sessions come up with brilliant product ideas from time to time. At Anheuser-Busch, it was the wholesalers who had the most influence in changing the Bud Light ad campaign to the (highly

• **Two examples of nostalgia licensing—Betty Boop charms and Coke wallpaper—show how old properties can be revitalized. Lesson: old trademarks should be studied, not kept in the company vaults.** (Betty Boop courtesy of Future Creative Art, Inc., ©1986 King Features Syndicate, Inc.; Coke courtesy The Coca-Cola Company.)

successful) ''Gimme a Light—a Bud Light'' from the unmemorable earlier effort—generated by creative types. At 3M, it was a secretary who invented their fabulously successful Post-it™ pads. Hostess Twinkies got their name from a sales rep who happened upon a shoe sign for ''Twinkle Toes.''

The moral, for senior executives: let your subordinates look around for licensing concepts that may, just may, work. Use your own contacts in other industries to explore cost-free ways to exploit new markets. The moral for others in the company: dare to be a little different; assume that, with encouragement from your superiors, you *can* generate licensing concepts that have a chance to work.

UNUSED OR WASTED ASSETS

At the heart of any successful licensing program is a detailed analysis of every nook and cranny of your business. Quick profits can be made with a single licensed product, but for a long-lasting program, you need to be completely aware of all the ways your company has failed to use its nontangible assets over the years. In a 50-year life of a company, if it fails to take advantage of every possible business opportunity within reach, it may have lost millions of dollars. On the margins—where most companies operate—that lost income could have meant the end of the company. How's that for an ''opportunity cost''?

Let's look at some examples of how companies can take advantage of profit opportunities in licensing. They can be minor efforts, like using print ad space more efficiently. Or they can be more significant methods, as with major licensing campaigns using, say, old corporate logos.

A great many major packaged goods companies pass up opportunities to use part of their packaging for coupon offers or promotions. Why not regularly use that package space to advertise the licensee's product–Oreo T-shirts, let's say? With a company of any size, to convert part of its package wrapper into an advertising vehicle—that perhaps millions of shoppers will see—is to add, *at no cost,* an incredible new media base. We don't mean to suggest that you clutter a wonderful package design with advertising. But for the most part, package designs are easily adaptable.

Another area with plenty of room, literally, for improvement, is *space ads*. Little harm can be done by adding a line in a product ad linking the brand to licensed goods. Rarely is it done. The same

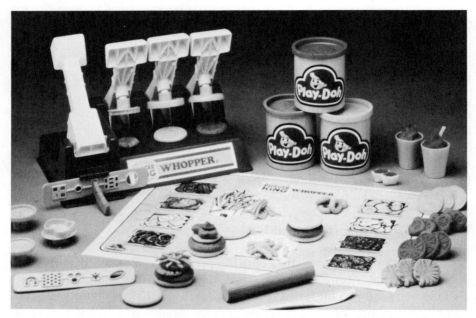

• **The licensee, Kenner Products, sees new life injected into a durable old toy, Play-Doh, with the help of licensor Burger King.** (Courtesy the Nancy Bailey Company.)

principle can apply to TV and radio spots. Often the brands' licensed product can be included; it seldom is.

Another asset many companies don't even consider developing is a *consumer mailing list*. Most companies that do develop them don't use them—they don't even rent them. How often, for example, have you bought an appliance, filled out the warranty card, and mailed it in, never to hear from the company again? Customer lists are a free way to hook loyal consumers into your licensing program, once launched.

At a major beverage company, thousands of consumer names and addresses were collected from cards "authenticating" each licensed item they purchased. These people were prime prospects for a follow-up catalog of licensed items. But for a time they were never mailed a catalog of any sort, so several hundred thousand dollars of profits were lost right there. The company now aggressively pursues mail-order customers with a catalog of its licensed items.

Some companies have benefited by using assets such as old logos, old classic print ads, items from their archives, and things of that nature. The Sporting News, for example, in the last few years has begun to dig out some of the precious gems in its 100-year-old archives. The

"Conlon Collection," baseball photos from the 1920s and 1930s, is the basis of a collector card series.

Coca-Cola and RJR Nabisco have used their *old logos* and *print ads* for licensed collector serving trays, tins, puzzles, prints, and even greeting cards. Anheuser-Busch's wooden miniature beer box on the Clydesdale hitch is one of their more successful licensed products.

Finding unused or wasted assets is part and parcel of real productivity improvement. Productivity improvement isn't merely a tough business analysis wherein a company's problems, such as labor waste and inefficiency, are rooted out. All that is good as far as it goes. But losses can be just as great when you have a product success that you don't capitalize on. Very few companies take the things they've *done right* and find ways to do *more* with them. Gallo's Bartles & Jaymes wine cooler is a good example.

You remember "Frank and Ed," who made this Gallo product the nation's best-selling wine cooler. Frank and Ed were minor cult figures. People talked about them at the office, at parties, just as they have more recently idolized Spuds MacKenzie. But Gallo did nothing (in contrast to Anheuser-Busch) to develop loyalty to the product by exploiting Frank and Ed's fame. Frank and Ed should have been pictured in special display stands across America. A clothing line could have been established. One can only guess at the number of Ed's overalls that might have sold, for example. But Gallo wasted the asset.

LEVERAGING YOUR "EQUITY"

Another way for the licensor to look upon the licensing program is that it is the ability to *leverage* intangible equities. If done shrewdly, this leveraging will put distance between your company and most others.

As licensor, you must have three capabilities working in concert:

1. You must understand the consumer's perception of your brand and company.
2. You must understand how your equity can fit with a licensee's business and help the licensee in its industry.
3. You must develop the concept so there is enough meat on the bone to attract the licensee.

So you must become familiar with the licensee's industry *and* with the specific licensee's company. You acquaint yourself with consumer usage and purchasing dynamics of the licensee's business and with the

* **The Keebler hollow tree cookie jar is an excellent "loop test" example. It gives the consumer another reason to buy the Keebler core product: to fill the cookie jar itself. Produced by licensee Nelson McCoy Pottery.** (Courtesy TLM Enterprises.)

distribution system (where applicable), profit margins, and the other ingredients in the given industry's profile.

Proof that your equity has been properly leveraged comes by administering what can be called the "loop test": Does the licensed item truly *support the licensor's primary product* and corporate or brand reputation? It isn't enough that the licensed product produces profits or gains exposure that would not have otherwise come; it must also redound to the benefit of the brand or corporation.

Lever Brothers' Snuggles Fabric Softener performs the loop test flawlessly with its Snuggles teddy bear, sold in retail shops. Obviously, the teddy bear reinforces the primary product's reputation as a truly effective softener.

Jim Beam Kentucky Bourbon now offers a bourbon cake mix, passing the "loop test" perfectly. It is a successful attempt on the part of the licensor to not only extend its brand's image beyond the market for the brand itself and into another consumer area, but to also strengthen the overall image of the product.

Another excellently conceived licensed product that passes the loop test and extends the image of the primary product is Hershey's chocolate milk. Hershey now has a significant piece of another section of the grocery store—the dairy section—and its chocolate candy's reputation gains an edge on the competition with a whole new group of consumers. They're predisposed to buying Hershey's chocolate bars.

We can't resist pointing out licensed products like Snuggles teddy bear, Jim Beam bourbon cake mix, and Hershey's chocolate milk to cautious potential licensors who worry, "Aren't we risking our brands by getting into licensing?" No. It's crucial to understand that unlike financial leveraging (which carries some risk), leveraging in licensing, if done properly (something you can measure *ahead* of the time the product is put on the market), *enhances* your brand name, thereby *reducing* dangers to it posed by competitors. What has Hershey's risked by bringing out chocolate milk? In Hershey, Pennsylvania, they're kicking themselves for not doing it decades ago.

Getting the most out of your "lost equity" ties in to productivity improvement—*positive* productivity improvement, with none of the bad connotations the term usually has within the company. And the net result will be as if you have reduced overhead or taken whatever other unpleasant steps are entailed in productivity improvement.

• Loop test: Jim Beam Kentucky Bourbon Cake, manufactured by licensee Downey's Products, is found in gourmet food shops and fine department stores. (Courtesy TLM Enterprises, licensing consultants for Jim Beam.)

CHAPTER 3

HOW TO LOOK AT YOUR COMPANY AND ITS UNTAPPED EQUITY

Let's explore your nonfinancial assets. How do you identify them, and how do you best use them in a licensing program? Outside the company, how are you and your brands perceived by consumers, retailers, and the competition, and how should you respond to their perceptions?

LOOKING FROM WITHIN

This part of the chapter will have five subsections: brand image, customer base, distribution, promotion potential, and expertise.

Brand Image

A licensor must first select those trademarks or brands deemed to have appeal among consumers. Before proceeding with licensing plans of any sort, the legal people must run a check on trademarks. Trademarks may, indeed almost certainly will, be protected in your core industry, but it is up to the lawyers to ascertain if anyone else in other product categories—or countries—is using the mark. This process will define *for* you how and whether you have "extendability" for a given brand. It might be tougher for some than others. Wonder Bread, for instance, has a more generic cast to it than does The Sporting News, which is a very specific and descriptive trademark. (A later section explains how licensing can actually work to build and protect the company trademark.)

Having finished the trademark/brand check, the licensor should

• **The venerable MGM/UA, with its lion, capitalizes on a pool of consumer goodwill it has filled over decades.** (Courtesy MGM/UA TM®.)

take stock of internal company opinion about the chosen brand(s). What kind of image does it have among the company's marketing people? It is hoped that this image coincides generally with consumer opinion, but it's also important to decide what kind of image the licensor wants to encourage consumers to have or develop in the future. (The licensing program should point in that direction, of course.)

Customer Base

This is the key equity a company "owns." A business that has financial backing and a great product idea, marketing plans, and distribution setups, still needs customers to succeed. Corporate America accordingly spends a great deal of time and money to understand the customer better.

Most companies succeed, at least mostly, in knowing their primary consumer, though certain kinds of companies tend to be better at this than others. Magazine publishers, for example, generally get a much closer fix on their customer, because they have to in order to convince advertisers to buy ad space. If *Newsweek* can show that 33 percent of their readers have personal computers, they might get IBM to buy an ad when their newest PC is ready.

Other kinds of companies may have a less complete consumer

profile—may in fact need to learn a lot more about this most important asset before getting into a licensing program. In order to attract a quality licensee, and in order to satisfy skeptics within the company itself, licensors should know their customer base inside and out. This knowledge is the most direct assurance a licensee, who is risking capital, can have about the direction your licensing program is taking. Does it make sense for, say, a packaged goods company to be in apparel licensing? The customer profile should give you solid assurances (but naturally, no guarantee of success) and the licensee reason to devote time and money to the enterprise.

Distribution

The distribution system for the licensor's core product must not be jeopardized by the introduction of a licensed product into the system.

A typical consumer products company that uses a distributor/wholesaler network to sell its core product to the retail trade makes relations with that network a constant preoccupation. (Anheuser-Busch treats its wholesalers like royalty; Lee Iacocca gave his dealers a trip on the QE II.) So if a company such as Hershey's can't get its licensee's product into major store chains without causing distraction, they shouldn't attempt to do so. Its distribution system, after all, is an *integral part* of the core product that makes Hershey a dominant candy company.

On the other hand, the mere potential for problems should not be identified as the problem itself. Bringing a licensee into the distribution network need not hurt anyone; it may even make everyone down the line very happy. For example, a licensee itself is quite capable of introducing a distributor to new promotional strategies in a local market. If, say, M&M chocolate bears greeting card display is introduced in a supermarket, M&M's distributor will reap the reward. M&M thereby has placed its trademark into another aisle of the store. You can bet more than one shopper has spotted the display and headed for the candy aisle (perhaps even to complement the greeting card with an M&M candy product).

Not incidentally, the licensor may find, having analyzed the distribution network, that it has a weakness that can be helped by linking up with a licensee. The ideal licensing program actually does strengthen the whole system while at the same time making the licensor no longer entirely dependent on the core product's distribution network. In the case of some companies (e.g., Calvin Klein or Ocean Pacific), that's

• Licensee expertise in packaging for retailers exhibited here with BIC's display case.
(Courtesy the BIC Corporation.)

important. These apparel makers have arranged a good part of their volume to revolve around licensing contracts.

Promotion Potential

This is one of the most fertile grounds from which to draw. But most of what follows requires that company decision makers shed some minor conventions. Most advertising agencies will frown, though not all of them. At least several agency executives agree with most of the ideas put forth below.

One of the most important marketing/management skills is knowing how to get the most out of advertising expenditures. A licensed product provides wonderful opportunities in virtually every area of promotion and advertising, including TV and radio; print ads; mailing lists and direct mail; promotional events and coupons; package space; and space ads.

I don't see these media being fully used, whether for primary product advertising or in licensing programs. I'll confine my comments to how each can be better used by the licensor and licensee.

TV

We've seen companies, most notably in major consumer-product businesses like the beverage industry, pass over countless chances to benefit their licensee *and* strengthen the commercial's appeal, too. As

McDonald's, Coca-Cola, and Coors have recently proven, one needn't clutter a commercial with licensed products in order to help out a licensing program and at the same time reinforce a brand image. All three of these major licensors now expertly use their own licensed apparel in commercials. I haven't noticed any marketing problems as a result. (The opposite, if anything.)

Many companies spend a good deal of money trying to place their products into major motion pictures. (Who at Miller wouldn't want to see Tom Selleck downing a Miller Lite?) So a first step is to get the most out of their own TV ads.

This holds particularly for those who use the less expensive videotape, as opposed to film, to produce the TV spots. Videotape makes it simple to add a five-second promo spot about a given licensee and product. Precious few licensors who advertise on TV are doing this. One who tested the idea: The Sporting News, for its Computer Baseball Game.

Radio

Because radio requires (more often than not) "live talent," ads can be altered weekly or even daily, plugging different special promotions based on licensed products. If a new licensee has a product but a limited advertising budget, radio may be just the medium. It is possible to tag along on the licensor's commercials by offering a free sample product or contest opportunity.

Print Ads

For companies that use print ads extensively, what harm, aside perhaps from upsetting some graphics people, can a tastefully added line of copy do to the ad's primary pitch? Why not give the consumer the name of a major retailer (Sears or Penney's) who carries your licensed product? Unless there's an extraordinary reason, product space ads with extra room could contain help for the licensee's product as well.

Mailing Lists and Direct Mail

If your company uses direct-mail advertising, you should be able to augment any licensing endeavor by announcing licensed products available to consumers through your licensees. You may also be able to defray your direct-mail cost by sharing this expense with the licensee or charging him a small "per thousand" fee for "piggybacking" the ad onto your direct-mail package. That's all a matter for negotiation.

Mailing lists of consumers should be offered as incentives or as extra promotion vehicles to the would-be licensee. The list should be offered to licensees at a healthy discount. Depending on the industry, the licensee may already do direct mail. That will benefit the licensor by, in theory at least, generating immediate royalty income. The licensor also derives modest list-rental income—while the licensee has an inexpensive prime list of consumers already somehow tied to the licensor's brand.

Promotional Events and Coupons

Most marketing managers are wary of this whole category. Promotions are off the beaten path, a great struggle to "pull off," generally. But a promotional event, even one organized around your primary product, can also be an opportunity for a licensee to officially promote his product. If the licensor is paying for the event, it is possible to negotiate a fee from the licensee. Some licensees, after all, may not be able to afford their own promotional events.

Coupons give the consumer a discount on the product; hence the bias against them. "Stay away from coupons unless forced to use them" is pretty much the marketing people's attitude.

But providing a coupon program for your licensees is an entirely new and inoffensive concept. Consider: The licensor isn't discounting the core product, but the response that can be generated by having the licensee use coupons for the *licensed* product amounts to almost the same thing. Wouldn't a coupon for, say, a sweatshirt, placed in a Wilson basketball package, only boost sales of Wilson's sweatshirts and other apparel in the licensed line? And wouldn't that all generate more enthusiasm for other Wilson products? Meantime, the licensor, Wilson in this case, assists the licensee in a major way.

Package Space

Most products have two kinds of packaging: the primary package (the container carrying the product) and the secondary package, or the outer box, carrying package, or whatever. More often than not, the secondary packaging provides space for promoting a licensed item. The promotion can be done effectively, without spoiling the aesthetic appeal of the packaging.

This package space can be a medium all its own, worth possibly millions of advertising dollars to a licensee. It is therefore a nonfinancial asset worth plenty to a licensor's bargaining position.

Even a smallish packaged goods manufacturer will put thousands of packages on store shelves every few days. The primary function of these packages while on the shelves is to be a billboard for the product. Let's take a hypothetical example: Kimberly Clark, makers of Huggies diapers, licenses its name to a maker of baby furniture. The side of the Huggies box is then reversed for a mail-order-style ad inviting mothers to write in for a catalog of furniture items their licensee offers. In no time, the licensee will have sold thousands of units; the catalog mailing list would number in the tens of thousands.

Space Ads

The last great unused promotional vehicle is exclusively for print publishers who sell advertising space. (The principles actually apply also to networks such as CNN or ESPN.) Such companies can, if they choose, enhance their licensing programs by allowing the licensees to use ad space at a discount, perhaps a deep discount.

The *per inquiry*, or PI, method, is the most workable; some variation of it might also work. The publisher would be paid per response, rather than receive a flat ad rate. Or, the licensee could guarantee the publisher's raw cost of the space plus a PI rate. For example, say *The Wall Street Journal* signs a licensing deal with an online computer company offering subscribers a financial advisory and news service for a fee. *The Wall Street Journal* gives their licensee a special PI rate—and makes money that way (per response) *and* through the royalty, anywhere from 7 to 33 percent, on the number of subscribers recruited by the licensee. Obviously, publishers will have to work out the numbers.We suggest that the concept should not be dismissed out of hand. Indeed, one licensor–licensee arrangement works precisely along these lines. Modified PI arrangements are a special service publishing licensors can provide licensees—and profit from it themselves.

Expertise

Expertise isn't always explicitly part of a licensing deal, but it comes with the package. Technical, marketing, distribution—all these areas of

---

• **Seven-Up's "Spot":** A unique attempt by a consumer products company to develop its own character, and thereby extend its trademark, based on its logo (notice the red spot between "7" and "UP"). Many licensees have joined the project with varied products, including: Applause, with "Spot" bendables; Franco Manufacturing, with beach towels; Nasta Industries, with sunglasses, bendables, and windup toys; and Commonwealth, with a "plush." (Courtesy the Nancy Bailey Company.)

(usually) licensee competence must be recognized by the licensor, who will in turn usually offer not only its name, but its consumer base, promotional efforts, perhaps its own distribution system. Both parties stand to benefit substantially. Using a corporate logo or trademark, in and of itself, will get no one beyond the planning stages. And the licensor, though not liable financially in the licensing arrangement, should realize that it has something beyond a brand name to offer the licensee.

FROM THE OUTSIDE LOOKING IN

Having completed a thorough review of the company with an eye toward finding hidden assets, the results must be cross-referenced with a clear knowledge of how the company and its brand image and/or trademark—in short, its equity—is perceived by those outside the company. There are three major elements on the outside to investigate: the consumer, the retailer, and the competition.

First, the *consumer*. What does he or she think of you and your product? It's common for companies not to fully understand their image. There is always a tendency to think that consumers' views coincide with the way the company promotes itself. But in undertaking a licensing program, the licensor must get as objective a consumer reading as possible. "Focus groups" are as good a way as any. There, companies can meet consumers loyal to their product (and it's important to meet consumers of other brands, for complete perspective). One important task at focus groups is getting your customer's viewpoint *both* on your company and on its individual products. This entails detailed questioning about past and current promotion and advertising. It's one thing to get a consumer impression about an ad; another, sometimes, to hear a view about the company itself. It's one thing, also, for a giant such as Anheuser-Busch to hear consumer views of its mass market product, Budweiser; another to hear them talk about a pricier product such as Michelob—and perhaps still another to hear views about the corporation itself.

Obtaining consumer views has a way of clearing company minds, sharpening its understanding of consumer preference, narrowing the odds that are generally stacked against a new product introduction or a licensed product idea. Moreover, consumer focus groups can add a whole new dimension, actually providing viable product ideas. These

• **Jack Daniel's Charcoal Briquets, introduced under a licensing agreement with Hickory Specialties, exploits not only a brand name that stands for high quality, but also a key part of the Jack Daniels manufacturing process. The briquets are from wood "barrels" used to hold the liquor being produced.** (Courtesy Equity Management, Inc., of Chicago, which manages the Jack Daniel's licensing program.)

are the folks, after all, who spend the money. They can tell us what they'll buy *and why*—and *that's* when you can draw out some new ideas. Getting the consumer perspective will also aid licensees. The information will help them plan marketing programs on which the success of the licensing program largely depends.

The beauty of focus groups is that for a few thousand dollars, a licensor can save millions. If a concept bombs among consumer test segments, it will almost certainly bomb in the marketplace. The converse isn't always true. Enthusiasm in focus groups isn't always a guarantee of success. But one always learns from them. If Coca-Cola had relied more on focus groups instead of just blind taste tests (two unmarked cups with New Coke and original Coke), would New Coke, the most widely publicized new product failure since the Edsel, have ever hit the supermarket shelves? Proper use of focus groups would have shown Coke just how much brand equity they'd accrued in the original brand.

Retailers constitute the second key element of the "outside" atmosphere. Consumers buy your product, but as any manufacturer knows, it's the retailer who must do the selling. What licensed products would the retailer like to see? What is the retailer's view of you and your

• **Nostalgia licensing—and a perfect fit for a character and a product: Howdy Doody watches.**   (Courtesy Concepts Plus, Inc.)

competition? In what areas would the retailer expect you to appear with licensed merchandise? In what areas would he or she expect you to be successful? Get answers from the retailer.

Beyond this, retailers themselves may have reason to welcome your licensed product. Retailers are always looking for ways to develop sections of the store that seem underused. Perhaps they need to develop a given area on the floor differently; or again, perhaps there's a new product category they can exploit. Whatever the case, if your company has good relations with retailers, you and your licensee can go to the head of the line when the time comes for retailers to make changes or additions and make new buys.

With "double clout" as a result of the licensor–licensee arrangement, you may find yourself chosen by a retailer ahead of another manufacturer who, operating alone, has identified the same product need that you and your licensee/licensor have seen. Except that you're better able to produce customers.

Which brings us to the third outside element, your *competition.*

Licensing provides your company with a potent added weapon to compete with. A licensing program can, if used properly, strengthen the position of the licensor's brand by generating items to flank the core product. A classic illustration of licensing's power is the way Coca-Cola used it—on apparel—at the beginning of the brutal Coke–Pepsi war. Pepsi was making inroads, but all of a sudden America saw that "new generation" of Pepsi kids . . . walking around in Coke rugby shirts and the like. Pepsi's licensing response didn't get off the ground until a couple of years later.

Just as there are many elements to business success, so it is with licensing. Understanding your consumer, the retailer, and the competition, rank highest on our list. And we should add another element: constant review of the first three by your company.

DEVELOPING WHAT YOU HAVE LEARNED

Once ascertaining what your hidden assets are and what the consumer and the retailer think of the company (not to mention what your competition's position is, and what they think of you), how do you use all the information initially? Obviously, it should all be gathered into a report, one distributed liberally around the company executive ranks— junior as well as senior. The licensing administrator should coordinate and oversee this process. All the reactions and ideas should flow through the licensing administrator's office, or else chaos might follow. The report would look very much like the one in Appendix B for a fictional major consumer products company.

With the overall company objectives for its core products ever in view, ranking company executives must commence the study of new licensing venture opportunities.

What Are the Major Problems?

Seek out all the major problems the company has encountered. In focus group research, did consumers point out things that worry the marketing people? Is there trouble with retailers for any reason? If the company has several products, which ones have a long life expectancy, and of these, which are weakest and which are strongest? What are your difficulties with your competitor? And what are the competitor's strengths and shortcomings? Once the problems and trouble spots are identified, it's time to generate solutions—as much as such can be generated—via a proposed licensing program.

Finding the Solutions

"Solution sessions" should be carefully planned meetings in which new ventures—licensing ventures—are proposed with the company's over-all strategy in mind. The meetings might take a period of weeks, and in a

• Via licensing, Nerds® has taken a (nonchocolate) candy that suffers in sales during the Easter season and made its product competitive at that very time. Sunmark, Inc., makes Nerds® and the licensee is Hinkle Easter Products. Alaska Momma,® Inc., is the licensing company.   (Courtesy Alaska Momma,® Inc.)

superficial way, they might resemble brainstorming sessions. But the solution sessions should be disciplined, not a free-for-all. On the other hand, people from all the company's divisions and departments should be on hand; junior- and senior-level people from every conceivable area, including accounting, manufacturing, even shipping. No more than 10 people at a time should meet, otherwise the discussion becomes unwieldy. If need be, have multiple sessions; the individual sessions should each finish in a few days.

Typically, a company tries to solve problems by using the resources immediately at its disposal—conventional weapons, if you'll permit. But *not* in these sessions. The company (i.e., the potential licensor) need not have expertise in an industry to match a licensed product suggestion someone has made. Nor does it need just the right distribution system or manufacturing plan. Nor is a budget necessary. These solution sessions should be free of all the worries that any of the company experts may have. In licensing, someone else handles the problems, not the licensor. This isn't to say that a company can do anything it wants in licensing, but in the beginning stages, it should

• **LifeSavers® apparel by Mayfair exploits not just the familiar trademark, but the color scheme and the actual "o" ring of the product itself.** (Courtesy Mayfair Industries.)

suspend the usual concerns in order to get every possible good idea on the table. Assume that the licensee will have to cope with most of the problems generally associated with a new product. That's usually the way it works, in a smoothly running program.

The three main criteria to establish when developing licensing ideas at this stage are:

1. The concept must be seen as reinforcing the core product.
2. It should have some value to the consumer in and of itself.
3. It should be attractive enough to licensees to get some of them interested in joining forces with the company (you must have reason to believe that you can find a licensee).

In order to best develop what you learned about the company's hidden equities, these solution sessions must see the participants crawl out of their company skins. It's proper that they normally think the way they've been trained and conditioned within the company, but it's not proper for these early licensing-idea sessions. They may generate hundreds of ideas, by the way. Then comes the task of choosing the best half dozen or dozen.

PICKING THE BEST LICENSING IDEAS

Broad guidelines can be given for narrowing down your list of licensing ideas, but no systematic formula. The licensor will have to rely in part on intuition and good marketing sense, and of course on focus groups. We do strongly advise that all concerned *resist* the urge to pare down the list of ideas to one or two. It's well to remember that new products, whether in licensing or not, don't always succeed. Indeed, the majority fail. While licensing doubles your chance of success (because you have two companies with the incentive and skill to make an item sell), you will need to have several irons in the fire to make all the effort worthwhile—and to get the most out of the licensing program. Each licensed item helps the licensor; and, since the licensor doesn't invest time and effort once the merchandise is produced (that's the licensee's task), why not have several items moving at once? That is one of the great advantages of licensing for the licensor, after all.

As for the selection process itself, take the list of licensed product ideas and put the concepts into various categories:

• **Collector tins, despite the fact that they are now commonplace, can be successful for brand name promotion and especially for a given property created by an individual artist expressly for licensing.** (Courtesy Cheinco Housewares, a division of Chein Industries.)

• **Smart licensing: Black & Decker products are purchased by adults, and a majority are males. With the licensed toy products, Black & Decker involves a young audience, predisposing the kids to either buy Black & Decker products when they grow up or at least have a favorable impression of the company.** (Courtesy The Black & Decker Corporation.)

- Good, better, best.
- Easiest to launch.
- Promotion/advertising potential.
- Consumer loyalty quotient.
- Fits well into the core product/corporate strategy.
- Brand equity is used to the fullest.
- Good chance to compete successfully with other brands.
- High royalty potential.
- Unique.
- Easily linked to a brand; will strengthen brand imagery.

The licensed product concepts should also be categorized by industry, and any industry that a licensor wishes to penetrate through licensing should be evaluated. You might commission a formal analysis, though it is not absolutely necessary at this stage. But do make a comprehensive review of each targeted industry, primarily through secondary sources. This can be done efficiently and without great cost, and it will provide a list of potential licensees in each industry. Just as important, it will reveal industry dynamics and new developments, rendering a better understanding of an area alien to your company.

CHAPTER 4

SETTING UP AND MANAGING A LICENSING DEPARTMENT

This chapter contains five sections: (1) defining the department's functions, (2) the ideal organization, (3) steps to start up, (4) finding the right talent, and (5) managing your licensing program.

DEFINING THE DEPARTMENT'S FUNCTIONS

A licensing department has five primary functions: (1) trademark protection, (2) image extension/expansion possibilities and review of unsolicited ideas, (3) licensee and product development, (4) licensing administration, and (5) retailer relations and promotions. Let's look at each one.

Trademark Protection

This is the most important function of them all. Often, corporate trademarks that companies have developed over the years—and have spent millions of dollars marketing—are not properly protected. This is usually the result of a very limited view of what that trademark has stood for, compounded by a too-limited use of the trademark. To be protected, trademarks must be *used*. If a company has no access to a particular product category, it is extremely difficult, if not impossible, to protect the company's trademark in that category. Licensing provides a vehicle by which to enter new categories. But along with this advantage comes the responsibility to *protect* that trademark when another operation or company infringes upon it. Your company must be willing to take to task, or to court, if necessary, organizations that enter a category that your licensee is in.

Along with trademark control comes the responsibility of setting up a method for catching infringers and a system by which they can be reported and dealt with. Most of the reporting will be done by your licensees. They have a vested interest in so doing, and they know their selling territory. They are most likely to catch any infringers first. Reporting can also be done by a company's distribution network or any other personnel within the company, however. On the next page is a sample "reporting form," exactly as it is written and distributed, courtesy of Major League Baseball®, which runs one of the best licensing operations anywhere.

There are three elements to effective trademark protection and control:

1. Keeping complete correspondence files regarding your relations with the licensee. A good filing system is critical because a licensor needs, at its fingertips, proof of intent to control and protect the trademark.

2. Having a clear plan of how approvals are given to licensees for licensed products, how they should submit both variations on these products and new ideas.

3. The licensing department must notify the legal department or company lawyers when different product categories are under consideration for licensed goods. The lawyers must clear the category for trademark use. For those who plan to do international licensing, it is essential that someone in the legal arm of the company registers the trademark in other countries—and does a trademark search in other countries as well.

Image Extension/Expansion Possibilities and Review of Unsolicited Ideas

Good licensing programs usually generate interest and a constant flow of business expansion inquiries from potential licensees and their agents, providing concepts and ideas to a licensor. Many ideas will sound attractive. However, they must be properly reviewed and analyzed with the image of the core product always in mind. And not just the image: advertising strategies and overall company direction must also be factored into judgments. But good licensing programs should generate concepts from *within* using results of research and the ideas of a company's most creative people. This fund of concepts will generate new licensees and enhance relations with existing ones.

Sample reporting form

MAJOR LEAGUE BASEBALL

RETAIL PRODUCT INFRINGEMENT REPORT

INSTRUCTIONS - PLEASE READ BEFORE FILLING OUT FORM

1. Provide as much information as you can. Major League Baseball cannot pursue suspected infringers unless we have adequate information. The more specific information we have, the faster we can take action.

2. Purchase a sample and send it along together with the packaging and wrapping material with the store receipt. You will be reimbursed. Major League Baseball cannot and will not take any specific steps against an alleged infringer unless we are provided a sample of the merchandise in question for evaluation.

3. Determine (if possible) who is the manufacturer of the suspected infringement and be sure to include that data on the form. We are most interested in eliminating infringements at their source. We prefer not to take action against any one retailer, distributor or jobber - they are only "the tip of the iceberg".

4. Include on the form as much detail as you can about the in-store selling environment. Is the suspected infringement being sold with officially licensed Major League Baseball items? Is there any in-store display material referring to the suspected infringement as "official"? Does the store manager or sales clerk remember the salesman of the suspected infringement saying anything that represented the product as being "official" or "okay to sell"?

5. Attach to the form as many pieces of tangible evidence (store ads, manufacturer's selling sheet, price lists, catalogs, etc.) relative to the suspected infringement. The more, the better; and such material can be extremely important in proving an infringement.

6. Send the form along with product samples and any supporting material(s) to:

> MAJOR LEAGUE BASEBALL
> 350 Park Avenue
> New York, New York 10022

ATTENTION: LEGAL DEPARTMENT AND EXECUTIVE VICE PRESIDENT OF LICENSING

Sample reporting form (*concluded*)

MAJOR LEAGUE BASEBALL

RETAIL PRODUCT INFRINGEMENT FORM

1. ITEM _____

_____
_____

2. WHERE PURCHASED
   A. Store Name _____
   B. Store Address _____

   C. Store Phone # _____
   D. Store Contact (Name) _____

3. DATE PURCHASED _____

4. MANUFACTURER OF INFRINGING ITEMS
   (Complete name and address of firm who manufactured suspected
   infringement. If manufacturer not available, please provide name
   and address of distributor or rep. supplying goods to retailer).
   A. Mfg. Name, if available _____
   B. Mfg. Address _____

   C. Phone # _____
   D. Mfg. Contact (Name) _____
   E. Rep. or Distributor, if available _____
   F. Rep. or Distributor's Address _____

5. RETAIL PRICE OF ITEM $ _____

6. SAMPLE ENCLOSED WITH STORE RECEIPT FOR REIMBURSEMENT Yes __ No __
   COMMENTS, IF ANY _____

7. OTHER INFORMATION - (Please provide as much detail as possible on:
   a) the amount of merchandise for sale, b) the number of separate
   infringing items (e.g., how many different items were represented);
   and c) the in-store merchandising and display of the merchandise.

8. ADVERTISING, IF AVAILABLE   Attached Yes __ No __
   _____
   _____

9. PRICE LISTS, BROCHURES OR CATALOGS, IF AVAILABLE
                                       Attached Yes __ No __
   _____
   _____

10. SUBMITTED BY:
    NAME _____
    ADDRESS _____

    PHONE # _____
    COMPANY _____
    DATE _____

Licensee and Product Development

This is like new product development, except that here we have new product development with two companies rather than with one.

In this case, of course, the products are licensed items. Therefore, they must fit the company's brand and strategy. Once it is decided that a given licensed product does this, a licensor must begin aggressive recruitment, finding the right licensee firms to enter into a partnership. In some cases, it may be wise to develop a potential licensee before the product concept is complete, thereby benefiting from a licensee's expertise. But whether a licensor selects the licensee before or after completing concept development, at some point the licensee and licensor will work together to refine the idea and get down to detailed product development.

It is also in this "research and development" stage that potential problems—at least, those that you can identify at this point—should be discussed. The licensor or licensee may wish to do consumer testing or focus group research. Even matters such as possible regulatory requirements must be looked into at this stage.

Licensing Administration

The head of the licensing department must make sure that the program is generating the maximum income possible from its ventures, that the performance of the licensee is monitored, and that the whole program also provides support to the trademark protection process and to the licensor's core product.

A continuing stable relationship with licensees is very important to the success of any licensing program. It is through the licensing administration process that regular communication with and control of the licensees takes place. With it comes new ideas for products and marketing, along with the troubleshooting so essential to the wellbeing of *any* business. With all this in mind the licensing administrator will tackle these specific tasks:

1. Quality control/plant inspection. The licensee should be told at the outset that the licensor will make unannounced plant inspections upon occasion. This should not trouble a licensee who is doing the proper job. He should welcome it.

A good way to ensure the highest possible quality for the licensed product is to do a product review of samples acquired in retail outlets or by the licensor's employees. What better way to check on the quality of a typical product produced by the licensee?

2. Financial review. Royalty reporting, on a regular basis, is a task that the licensee must perform scrupulously. The licensor should insist on that. A proper royalty review system is essential because it keeps the licensee relationship honest (no good licensee will object to it). It also helps the licensor's accounting department to get its own "handle" on the licensing department.

3. Contract monitoring. The major questions an administrator will ask here are: Is the licensee staying in the territory or category assigned? Is the licensee making the product exactly to specifications? (The latter is something you cannot always ascertain simply by inspecting a plant or purchasing a sample.) Does the artwork, if any, or the product itself, have the proper trademark registration?

Retailer Relations and Promotions

There can be cases where the licensor, rather than or in addition to the licensee, might be required to coordinate with the retailers to ensure the success of a given program. Good retailer relations are key to a company's business, and in licensing, good relations with retailers will support the program. Sometimes the licensor will help the licensee in this area, but it can happen the other way around as well. Spuds MacKenzie shops in Macy's came because of licensee clout, for example. Coke's apparel licensee got them point-of-sale displays that Coke couldn't have dreamed of otherwise.

Moreover, if the licensor is licensing a brand or trademark in a totally new and different distribution network and, because of the licensee, develops good retailer relations, this can provide the groundwork for a *new* core product entry in this same area. For example, McDonald's first made its way into Sears with apparel. Now, they're bringing restaurants into Sears stores.

Finally, and importantly, retailers with whom you have good relations can help you catch trademark infringers. For example, Sears will call licensors to make sure that an item is properly licensed before putting it into their catalog.

THE IDEAL ORGANIZATION

This section comes in two parts: (1) Positioning licensing in the corporate structure, and (2) intra-company relationships.

The Corporate Structure

It is crucial that the licensing department report directly to a top decision maker in the company. In a small company the owner or president will be the decision maker. In a larger company, the president reporting to the chairman of the board, or at least a vice president in the upper echelons, should oversee the licensing program. The chairman of the board should have at least an understanding of where the licensing program is headed and what its intent is. Licensing should be viewed as a major business management function and should therefore be on a par with marketing operations as well as with all the other main divisions of the company. Licensing should be given separate attention; *not* as a subpriority of marketing or the legal department, but as a separate mission.

The critical reason for licensing's independent position in the company is that it will affect many areas. It will support some areas, require support from some other areas, and become a vehicle to undertake independent projects. Licensing will mean diversifying, expanding, and innovating. And those three cannot be fit into any one area of your company.

Intra-company Relationships

Licensing will touch many departments in a company as it operates day to day. Let's first look at the legal department and the licensing contract. The **licensing and legal departments** must work hand-in-hand. In the area—the rather technical area—of trademark protection and control, the rest of the company, especially the licensing staff, must mirror the wishes of the legal department. In any trademark lawsuit, the licensing and legal people must work closely, compiling all the necessary evidence and the proof that the company has controlled and protected its trademarks systematically.

In addition, close cooperation between the legal and licensing departments will facilitate the (lawful) extension of trademark use into other categories. As each new licensee comes aboard, the legal department should be given all the necessary proof and evidence needed to expand the trademark into new categories.

The most important element of a licensing agreement is, of course, the contract itself. In Appendix A you will find the best (generic) licensing contract that we have ever seen. Not surprisingly, it's written by the Grimes & Battersby firm. There is also commentary attached to it. For our purposes here, we'll list the attributes that the best licensing contracts have:

1. They are easy to read. Anyone in business should be able to grasp most of the particulars of a typical licensing contract. Each section of a good contract should be subheaded. The contract itself should be arranged so that it is easy to browse through. The licensing contract will have to be referred to continually during a licensor-licensee partnership. It will be the control mechanism for both parties.

2. The contract should also incorporate elements that the *licensee* thinks he needs to be successful.

3. As trademarks are licensed worldwide, the legal and licensing departments need to work closely to establish the trademarks on the world market as well as to write contracts that are workable to people who speak other languages and come from other cultures. This generally requires legal counsel from lawyers in those countries.

4. Contracts should also carefully list what trademarks are to be used—and exactly for what purposes and what licensed items.

5. Most importantly, the contract should be made as much like a business document, rather than a legal document, as possible. The biggest problem with most contracts in licensing is that they tend to be so legalistic that the business people involved must run to their lawyers at every turn. That need not be the case. The licensing people in a company should be able to pull out the contract at any time and use it as a guide in dealing with the licensee. The licensee should be able to do the same with the licensor.

The **marketing department's** main function is, of course, product or brand management. Licensing people should have a complete understanding of the marketing plans and strategic direction for each brand—particularly those that have a potential to be licensed. Once they understand the current thinking of each brand group, the licensing people can launch diversification efforts via licensing that will strengthen and correctly portray an image of a given brand.

The licensing department should also itself be a source of new product ideas—products that can *either* be produced inside (and therefore become more of a new product management project) or done outside through licensing, or perhaps as joint ventures.

It's equally important that licensing and salespeople work well together. Sales efforts, after all, are directed ultimately at retailers. Moreover, licensed products *always* support the core sales effort of the company and can be marketed toward the retail trade. And from the sales department's point of view, they've got more news, more things to talk about with the retailer, when they can offer licensed products; the retailer, as any salesperson knows, should be shown all the advantages that you offer over the competition.

The **sales department** will be a great source of reporting about what your company's competitors are up to, particularly regarding new products. If the company can't react quickly enough to its competition's new product, it may be able to attack via licensing. It's not a panacea. It's not the way to overtake a rival (usually). But licensing is a viable response to problems presented by the competition.

The sales department might also be able to create products in tandem with the licensing department. Salespeople know, perhaps better than anyone else, the kinds of products that would be attractive on the retail level but are not possible to produce within the confines of their company. That's where licensing comes in; so salespeople and licensing people are made for each other.

With regard to sales promotions efforts, if the sales department is planning an event for promotion, several licensees may wish to join in to strengthen that promotion. Perhaps they could add promotional dollars or product offerings; or, the licensees might wish to become suppliers of merchandise to be given away.

The next area to discuss is **advertising**. There's a great deal to integrate between advertising and licensing. Licensing can increase the value of almost any advertising a great deal if the coordination is properly worked. It can also provide new dimensions to the advertising by carrying it from the medium it was designed for into different areas, for added promotion at no additional cost. Indeed, advertising can at times be paid for directly from the royalties it will generate from your licensed items. Slogans, images, overall campaigns—all can be useful to the licensing department. For instance, graphic illustrations that are done in print may become posters through licensing. A wealth of material like this goes only partially used in most companies. Many advertising agencies do a great deal of marvelous work that is put on the bench and never gets into the game. This kind of material, the "unused" stuff, if shared with the licensing department, could turn into extra revenue centers for the company. At the very least, such material might serve as extra promotional vehicles that cost nothing.

A great example of this is the Bud Light–Spuds MacKenzie phenomenon. The millions of dollars that were generated from exposure and sale of Spuds licensed merchandise were a great asset to the advertising campaign for Bud Light, and produced profits all around for the licensor and the licensee. The real opportunity is to turn these temporary media exposures—be it through TV, print, or radio—into permanent exposures. Spuds (or whatever) on sweatshirts, or turned into gift items, can become permanent pieces of advertising in consumer households. Although no one can put a number on the kind of free exposure a good licensing program can provide, we certainly can find examples of how best to generate unpaid-for media time/space.

Even the **accounting department,** specialized though it is, can lend a big hand in the licensing effort. If there is an audit to be done of a licensee (and by contract, an audit can be done almost any time), the licensing people must have the support of the accounting department. Second, it is up to the accounting department to see to it that the licensing department has set up proper royalty reporting mechanisms. The accounting department must also monitor that royalty reporting. Third, accounting should help to analyze a licensee, in detail, before any agreement with the licensee is reached.

A few brief words are needed about the **quality assurance department,** if a company has such a division. Particularly in the food-to-food licensing area, the standard of the product must be high. Safety standards, shelf-life requirements, transportation standards—these must be rigorous. Strictly speaking, this is not an intercompany matter. Nonetheless, a good relationship should be built between the quality assurance department of one company and the quality assurance department of another.

Inside the company itself, a good example of quality assurance cooperation with the licensing people is the practice in some beverage companies. They will test every drinking receptacle that is to have their logo on it and see how the taste of their beverage is affected by the receptacle before allowing the proposed deal to go through.

The **research and development department** can have a mutually beneficial relationship with the licensing department. A licensor's research and development people, on the one hand, will have opportunities to assist in making licensing ideas come true and, on the other hand, they might well get the chance to license some of the technology the licensor has developed. If the licensee is big enough to also have research and development people, then the two R&D departments could themselves generate new ideas, and perhaps even spin off a new business. For example, suppose a shoe manufacturer has an idea for longer-lasting rubber, and works with The Goodyear Tire & Rubber

Company to bring it to perfection. Their tennis shoe carries the Goodyear logo—let's call it the Goodyear Tennis Shoe.

In larger firms, the **acquisition department** should get involved in licensing. (So should investment bankers.) When a company is to be acquired, the licensing people and the acquisition people should look at it from a licensing perspective in addition to everything else. What about exploiting the nonfinancial assets of the new company? What can be done that is not being done with them? How can business be expanded *without* financial investment? Can a leveraged buyout be done to truly get the most out of the assets—the licensable assets? All of these factors are usually looked at in a half-hearted way (if at all), because the licensing expertise simply does not exist within many corporations to look at assets and ask, "What else can we get out of this company?" Here, the licensing department can provide a great service to the acquisitions department.

Let's look at a hypothetical example. Suppose the WD-40 Company, the relatively small producer of lock deicer and lubricant spray, is bought by General Motors. GM finds that loyal WD-40 users have a strong attachment to the product, which they rely on when the car or home locks cause trouble. This kind of intangible equity built up by WD-40 over the years, GM decides, could be put to use in the mechanics and tough-to-clean laundry markets. WD-40 soap, WD-40 laundry detergent—"To unlock tough dirt and stains."

As for the licensor's **public relations department,** it can offer a licensee a ready-made communications network with which to spread the news about the new licensed item. And the licensor can benefit from targeted industry public relations (PR) provided by the licensee in *its* industry.

Thus would the ideal licensing program run. The company leaders would understand its importance and potential, while all other divisions in the company would cooperate with the licensing people to extract the maximum benefits that licensing can provide.

STEPS TO START-UP

There are eight main categories to starting a licensing program: (1) reviewing equities, (2) licensing administration setup, (3) licensing concept generation, (4) research, (5) graphic development, (6) products/licensee development, (7) market development, and (8) pull-through programs. I'll explain the basic ingredients in each of these and show what must be done to get a licensing operation off the ground and moving. A bit later in this chapter, we'll explore what will be required for the long-term management of a licensing program.

Reviewing Equities

This entails an audit of past and present trademarks, photographs and drawings, and whatever else is available to the company that could provide material for a licensing program. This review can be divided into three sections: general review, legal review, and target consumer review.

General Review

This is a broad review undertaken to understand the history of the company and its past and present properties, and to identify all potential material that may be applied to licensing. All the materials will be categorized according to whether or not they have great, modest, or merely limited licensing potential. For example, nostalgia items will have limited potential because they often fit into a specialized, collectibles market. Current trademarks usually have more broad appeal, on the other hand. They might be categorized as having either great or modest potential.

Legal Review

All licensing material must be screened to determine legal rights the company possesses over the properties. First, each trademark should be evaluated to determine if the proper registration has been maintained and the trademark is current. Second, it must be determined if additional trademark classifications in other categories of use need to be registered to protect its use. The licensing and legal department should work together to strengthen the overall trademark position of the company's major brands and trademarks beyond their present-use categories.

Target Consumer Review

Though licensing provides the company's marketing program with the opportunity to expand its reach to consumers beyond the primary buyers of the product, still its primary responsibility remains to strengthen the company relationship with its target market, the consumer base we have mentioned before. It is important for the licensing management to understand, therefore, the full scope of marketing efforts, specifically the parameter of the target market and the psychographic and demographic compositions of the target consumer.

Licensing Administration Setup

Correct licensing management demands continuous analysis of the licensee's performance in the areas of quality assurance, trademark protection, royalty payments, and development of the contract. Since there is risk in permitting an outside organization to use a registered trademark, the licensing management system is there to provide comprehensive oversight.

Quality control standards must be set and maintained in order to prevent deterioration of the hoped-for image. Anything less than optimum image exposure would be a negative contribution to the company and should not be tolerated.

Procedures for an extensive product business review for quality, safety, and all potential legal liabilities, should be established and documented, and then incorporated into the licensing agreement itself. In addition, the promotional efforts that accompany the product or the business need the licensing management's attention. Since the company producing the advertisements is not the owner of the trademarks, it should be mandatory for the trademark owner to strictly control the trademark literature that uses its logos and brand names. Through this control the exposure can be fine-tuned to a company's exact specification.

The next area of the licensing administrator's duties is *trademark protection,* the foundation on which the licensed merchandising concept must be constructed. The requirements for trademark protection are:

1. Expertise in trademark law. If that does not exist within the corporate legal department, it must be obtained, either by hiring someone or going outside to a firm that knows the field.
2. An identification program that each licensee will institute to safeguard against infringers. This entails putting a line of copy on the package, label or ad that explains that the item is a licensed product of the licensor. Make it official, in short.
3. A broad-based system and active participation by which to locate infringers in the marketplace. Once infringers are located,

a series of methodical legal steps must follow to effectively protect the trademark: First, send a notice to cease and desist to the infringer and then file suit, after having made sure you have the documentation to back up your case. Licensed merchandise without a strong trademark protection policy is a fast way to cheapen the value of your properties and hurt your company image. Loss of reputation among your own licensees, not to mention the lack of concern you show, severely weakens your position for future legal bouts with infringers.

The next component in licensing administration is *royalty monitoring*. Licensing represents a sizable potential of revenue for a company, therefore proper royalty contribution systems must be developed. Delinquent reporting of royalties on the part of the licensees can deteriorate the marketability of company-licensed properties and substantially handicap the trademark protection component of the licensing effort. To wit, if you show lack of concern about getting paid, that's tantamount to saying—and the infringer will contend this—that you only care about exposure and free advertising. Which itself is tantamount to saying to a licensee that you won't fight infringers.

More than one licensor company, after raising royalty demands and tightening the trademark protection system, has noticed a heightened interest by licensees.

Royalty Reporting

Key elements of the "royalty reporting form" every licensor should provide a licensee are:

1. The name of each trademarked item being sold.
2. The product's description.
3. Wholesale sales figures: (*a*) number of units sold @ (*b*) wholesale price per unit.
4. Inventory on hand at end of reporting period.
5. Total sales.
6. Total wholesale dollars generated (× the royalty rate).
7. A section for any explanatory notes to cover any problems or surprises.
8. A line to be signed *by a chief financial officer of the company.*

Licensing royalties are based on the *wholesale,* not the retail, price.

A point-by point development of the licensing agreement or con-tract is important because it is the contract that will detail the working relationship between the licensee and the licensor. This document must therefore provide clear direction regarding all elements of the relation-ship. Appendix A is what we consider the finest basic licensing contract that has ever been drawn up, and we urge you to study it. There are comments accompanying the contract.

Licensing Concept Generation

Before developing licensing ventures, a company should undertake a licensing idea-generation session of probably a few days' length that includes several members of the company from all divisions. The purpose: to explore the various image-extension concepts worthy of licensing development. With your conclusions drawn, you will then seek out licensees (not waiting for them to come to the company) who will bring the idea(s) to light. To get the most out of the session, it should be organized in a professional way, generally using outside consultants in the "concept-generation business" to structure it and run the show. Principally, you will be seeking to establish areas of interest, often looking at the same time for basic company problems that need solving—and then trying to find as many solutions as possible through licensing. Therefore, one might almost call these sessions "solution sessions."

Research

The object of research is to get the consumer viewpoint about product ideas that are generated in the licensing concept-generation session. It is also important to get a clear understanding of the perception consumers have of the company name and its brands. The consumers themselves may be a great source of idea generation, either directly or indirectly, because they can look without vested interest at the licensor's brands and company name (*and* the competition's). Their lack of business sophistication is precisely what frees some of them to think of new products that they feel fit the image of a particular brand name or company.

Ideally, a potential licensor should conduct consumer focus groups where the analysis of the potential of the brand equity and company image is explored, and concepts are presented to consumers to get immediate response from them. Immediate, because it is important to get first impressions of a particular concept before consumers have a chance to think too much about it, thereby giving the opposite response from what is natural to most buyers: impulse. Smaller companies, where market research is an expense they generally cannot afford, need *not* conduct it in a formal way. But it is important that management of the company seek out, in some way, consumer opinion, even if only getting reaction from salespeople, retailers, even perhaps relatives and friends. A company that misperceives itself and diversifies by introducing new products based on the misperception (as mentioned in the case of New Coke) pays a heavy price for inadequate consumer research.

A major goal in consumer research is to determine exactly how consumers "feel" about the company and how they view the company in relation to its competition. Take terms such as *quality, safety,* and *fun,* and have consumers put concrete meaning to them. When you use your company's intangible equities in a licensed item, you use them in a way that jibes with consumer attitudes.

Such terms as *quality* can be interpreted in different ways. It is important that these abstract terms be defined by consumers as much as by anyone else that you might ask, such as company employees. For instance, quality at Anheuser-Busch is a sacred word. But its mainstay, Budweiser, is not the most expensive beer on the market, so quality certainly does not mean expensive. But in the case of Budweiser, it does mean that consumers *respect* and somehow feel comfortable (they are assured of real value) with the name.

That said, consumer views of new concepts, while important, are not the be-all and end-all. A licensor should also make sure the licensing programs/image extension efforts strengthen the core business. It is very dangerous to extend a particular trademark through licensing for the sole reason that it generates extra dollars, for example.

It's also beneficial to get retailer reaction for proposed licensing projects. Retailers will be the initial "consumers" of most items. We're talking not only about general merchandise stores but also about their equivalent in service industries. Retailers should be asked whether or not your concepts make good sense, how they believe they will be able to sell the product, and whether or not they will support it. For instance, if a consumer product company has particular items that can be licensed to another food category—Hershey into chocolate milk, Oreo into the ice cream section—it would be wise to check with, in these cases, the distribution system of retailers who already carry the primary product, to see if they would be open to such a brand extension. Not only can

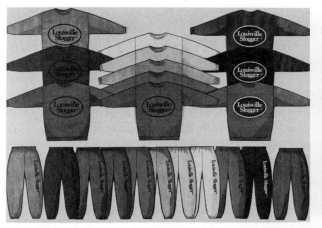

•Two different forms of trademark enhancement. Subject: the Louisville Slugger® logo, commonly seen on baseball bats. (Courtesy The Jathy Collection, Inc.)

they give you a quality critique of the concept, but they may be able to guide your development in such a project so that it would be a better fit in the distribution system.

There *are* checks and balances that make the licensing administrator's job less pressure-packed. Obtaining consumer and retailer opinions are perfect examples of this.

Graphic Development

Graphic art is the tool for licensees to use for guidance in reproducing the brand logos or trademarks. A licensed product can be made more marketable by a good graphics effort—for example, the ability to surround or enhance the core trademark in graphic situations that put forth a clear understanding of the image. There are two ways for graphics people to approach the process. The first may be called *trademark enhancement*. Here, the artist takes the basic logo and embellishes it by using special effects such as shadowing, outlining, or shading. The basic trademark is not changed. It is slightly altered to differentiate its use on the licensed item. On the other hand, the integrity of the trademark must be kept in order to ensure (legally) that it has been established in a proper way in a new category; and also to ensure continuity between the core product and the licensing program.

There are good examples of trademark enhancement in the apparel industry. Almost all licensees who have moved into that industry—for example, Wilson's Sporting Goods (sports gear)—uses exciting graphics associated with the product name.

The second and most effective (but more complicated) method is a process that might be known as *trademark transformation*. For instance, Budweiser means much more than a beer brand. It means, because of licensing, different things to a lot of different people. The apparel portion of the Anheuser-Busch program has been very successful because the graphics used on apparel took the Budweiser name and placed it within "sports situations"—whether surfing or auto racing, or softball—which imply that the trademark expresses a kind of solidarity with the types of experiences that Budweiser drinkers enjoy most. And they wear Bud apparel to signify their brand loyalty. (In fact, probably 10 or 20 percent of the Bud apparel wearers don't drink the brand.) Some licensing specialists refer to this as "lifestyle licensing." This is where logo or trademark transformation works to a tee.

Product and Licensee Development

Next: locating licensee companies who are interested in doing business with the licensor and qualified to use the licensor's trademarks and properties. Licensing provides the opportunity for the licensor to begin this search on several industry fronts at once—which is good, because there will be some concepts that fall by the wayside, leaving a few on which to concentrate. One comforting factor for those nervous about getting into anything too quickly is that in these early stages, not only does the licensor have to be convinced that a concept is a good one, but so does the licensee. Two heads are better than one, and they'll often prevent hasty entry.

Simply because one can proceed on several fronts at once does not mean that the approach is helter-skelter. Indeed, focus is necessary. Concepts that have been generated should be put on a priority scale, and, depending upon the criteria that a company sets for diversification efforts, a systematic approach should be undertaken. Identify the industry in which the concept will be targeted. Then, an appropriate industry survey should be taken to determine the dynamics of the industry, the trends that are moving or shaping it, and the companies that may like the concept proposal.

Among the important criteria to use when selecting a licensee company is that the company should possess quality products that match the quality of the licensor. Business reputation in any kind of partnership is important. A company joining with another is going to share the reputation they both create. This is a risk from the licensor's perspective. But a careful analysis of the licensee's business practices (having been made before any agreement is signed) should allay the risk considerably, or nullify it altogether. Stability on the part of the licensee is also important. The licensee need not have been in business for decades, or have paid off every dollar it owes. But the licensing venture must have suitable financing, or the company must at least be in a position that prevents its business practice from being compromised if the licensing venture does poorly.

A Successful Launch

One of the most successful licensees around was launched in the early 1980s—a company called Berco. They were a small firm put together by an entrepreneur named Trevor Cohen to manufacture and distribute beer-can cigarette lighters. That's a pretty insignificant item; but this small company approached a big-name consumer-product company with impressive credentials and a worthwhile, professional business plan, together with suitable bank financing. They brought with them a successful track record in Europe, though they had only recently moved into the U.S. market. Their financial statement, however, was unimpressive, being a tiny company just beginning on a new continent. Nonetheless, in one year they had become one of the most successful licensees the big-name licensor dealt with. And with the credibility of the licensor and its brand name on Berco's product, they were successful in later acquiring a major test and follow-through sell program for their lighters at K mart. They have since built a large gift distribution business in Canada.

The moral: When looking for suitable companies as licensee partners, look at them in much the same way an investment banker looks at a company. The licensee will be getting a huge loan—the loan of the licensor's reputation. Just as banks and venture capital groups lend out money to individuals who have good credentials and good ideas but not the hard financing, so also a good company licensing management group will deal out from their vaults a commodity just as valuable: its company image.

There is nothing in the world wrong with cultivating "big-company licensees," perhaps some of the leaders in a particular industry. They provide certain assets, both financial and nonfinancial, that are attractive. With such licensees, however, it is important to understand where they rank in their industry. A number-three ranking company that has a very stable business but may be looking for a competitive edge (to compete with numbers one and two) may be more enterprising and hungry for success. They'd be your best bet.

Upon selecting a few finalists, it is important for the licensor to do some homework to learn about the licensee's history, product line, its size and recent growth or decline. It is also good to learn about the company personnel on the upper levels and the internal environment. Oil and vinegar don't mix, nor do certain companies.

Even when a concept has been developed and the licensee has been picked, the process of developing the business relationship itself really is only just beginning, and many licensing ventures break down because the business relationship has not been structured with sufficient care.

Obviously, when two companies get together from two different industries, communicating can be a big problem. Each may talk a very different language. The same term can mean two different things. If you have experience in a big corporation, you know that even within two different departments of the same company, you may find a different language spoken. This all must be nipped in the bud.

The best policy when beginning to develop these business relationships is to get as much information on the table quickly, honestly, and with precision. Let the chips fall where they may. It is better that a licensing program fail early on than for it to be disrupted later.

It is the responsibility of the management of the licensing program to present in a straightforward way the components of the program and the licensor's expectations, and also to solicit the expectations and the worries honestly from the licensee.

A Continuous Development Process

As for the product development process itself, there are two tasks. First, develop a product that will capitalize on the equities of the licensor and the abilities of the licensee. Second, structure this product development process so that it will be a continuous development process over a period of years.

Licensing programs undertaken to produce one single product are *usually* both shortsighted and ill-conceived. When dealing with trademarks and brand images that have had a long life span (or at least have grown in popularity or established a reputation), it's important that the products which are developed in the licensing process fit into a company's *long-term* new products plan. It can be damaging to bring out a *single* product and after that product has run its life cycle remove

in the company, there are other abilities required of a licensing division head. They are listed here and then each one is explored individually:

1. New product, new business development skills.
2. Aptitude for contract negotiating.
3. Strong administrative talent.
4. Broad business background.
5. Ability to get along with people.

New Product or New Business Skills

Anyone involved with entrepreneurial ventures or products in a large corporation knows that this is an area supported by a great deal of business skill, but it is also an art. Entrepreneurs, and companies that have been successful in developing new products, have certain qualities. In general, they are hard driving and do their homework before jumping into a situation. The company itself seeks to provide a comfortable environment to nurture new ideas, encouraging personnel to take calculated risks after having investigated concepts. Finding someone willing to take risks, whether the person has made mistakes in the past or not, is a good first step for the licensor.

One danger for bigger licensor companies is that senior management might tend, having been groomed in mass-marketing techniques exclusively, to look down on relatively small operations or brand new ideas. All licensing programs are small and new in the beginning, so there's a built-in problem here.

Aptitude for Contract Negotiating

A hard-nosed type who relishes negotiation and loves to outsmart competition is by no means what a licensor needs. In fact, in good licensing relationships *both* licensor and licensee must "win." One of the quickest ways to snuff out a promising licensing effort is for the licensor to overnegotiate and try to get too much from the potential licensee. A truly good negotiator understands the *needs* of his counterpart, and takes them into account along with his own.

Each contract with each licensee will surely be different. Be as flexible as possible with them. There are of course certain things that the licensor cannot give away—maybe an untouchable logo or product. But remember that one set of terms may work for one industry while another set might be necessary for another industry.

Strong Administrative Talent

As noted earlier, good administration is the key to the licensing department. Indeed, it's really the key in any kind of new product venture. Keeping track, getting things done, motivating the individual and (in this case) licensees to make the process work—all of these things are necessary.

A lot of the licensing administrator's time will be spent in structuring business relationships and making sure they continue to operate smoothly. This involves a great deal of detail and follow-up. *Persistence* comes in handy for building the contract relationship, the actual product development, the marketing support assistance, the quality control, standards and reviews, the royalty reporting relationship—all the things required in a licensor–licensee relationship. Even with strong administrative skills, a licensing program will inevitably run into many minor difficulties simply because of all of this detail work.

Broad Business Background

A broad business background or the ability to understand other businesses will stand the licensing administrator in good stead. He or she will be dealing with many strange and unique companies and industries. The greater the knowledge and appreciation of how these different industries operate, the more likely it is that the licensing administrator will make good deals and associations that will thrive. A real bonus: an administrator having a small business background somewhere in the recent or distant past—it doesn't matter which. This guarantees hands-on experience and an acquaintance with high-pressure, day-to-day struggles for survival. And that, in turn, implies a willingness to roll up the sleeves and drive the licensing program to success.

Ability to get Along with People

Admittedly, this is almost purely a subjective evaluation. But the licensing administrator would need to function well under circumstances that might not always be pleasant. It helps if he doesn't fly off the handle or lose patience quickly. Moreover, an uptight administrator might cause relations with the licensee—a business partner, after all—to sour. Which would be a shame, because if the two parties in a licensing arrangement are honest and can exchange ideas and thoughts and concerns, that will make all the difference, assuming the product concept is a good one to start with. Communicating in business is not simply the ability to write letters or speak clearly. These are vital; but also important is the ability to take the bad news well (and to deliver it when necessary).

MANAGING YOUR LICENSING PROGRAM

We'll divide this section into three parts: (1) setting priorities, (2) pitfalls to avoid, and (3) growth and how to handle it. Our primary focus will be on applying the tools already set up in the licensing department. The day-to-day management approach that you take, and the avoidance of common pitfalls, will make the difference between a strong and a weak program.

Setting Priorities

This task is part and parcel of a succinct and clear statement of mission for the licensing program. Your purpose must be understood and communicated *before* you start. And while a company can begin with a broad investigation into licensing possiblities, it should be made clear to all concerned that at some point during this investigation, your focus will narrow as marginal ideas are cleared away. It is at this point that the company should begin to see licensing as an independently operating division with its own purpose, one distinct from other mainline company functions. Although working in concert with them, the licensing department cannot be smothered by other divisions.

Specific performance criteria should be set that can measure the broader goals of the program (the goals, to reiterate: protecting the trademark/brand name and broadening exposure of same; and financial success). The criteria are: (1) the number of licensees, (2) targeted industry categories, (3) projected royalties, and (4) a diversification plan.

Also, you must set a timetable in order to encourage a methodic and efficient—in short, a businesslike—approach. The biggest danger in licensing programs is a tendency for its managers to be somewhat undisciplined, at least compared to the rest of the company's executives. It's a natural enough tendency, given the overabundance of ideas and ways to bring them to fruition, but a firm administrator will have to ride herd on the staff as a result. There is a typical licensing plan in Appendix B that illustrates the correct approach.

There's a temptation faced by most licensing administrators once the licensing plan has been set in motion: to deviate from it for this or that reason. Often, the reason is that there's some "great opportunity" that they're convinced they must act on quickly. Often, a licensee has been lined up to further entice the licensor, and a plan for execution of the "great" concept is presented as well.

Another problem faced by some administrators is generally not of their making. A licensing department is established, standards and procedures for operating are developed and set, but the company holds back on research and testing of licensed product concepts. One might (correctly) say that this is a problem of the will, that a company setting up a licensing department which then drags its feet suffers from a kind of split personality. But that shouldn't be the final word. Were the company to solicit the help of professional marketing people, if need be, to guide them in research and testing, the whole situation could change dramatically. This kind of professional advice brought into the company becomes a catalyst for new ideas, and an objective voice that gives added confidence to even the most cautious executive. *Any* executive will need help when exploring ideas that will affect so many different parts of a company; this sort of thing always generates skepticism, or even resistance, in the early stages *within the company itself.*

A final important guideline for a licensing manager: Remember that in traditional new product development, your company has a great deal of hands-on control, but with development of licensed products, you have very little. Yes, there is *contractual* control. But there's no hands-on management for the execution of the concept. So all the criteria for execution must be made clear, and the licensor should establish a system to ensure that the criteria are met.

Pitfalls to Avoid

The licensing administrator will face other challenges, perhaps posed (inadvertently) by other company executives who don't know licensing, perhaps brought on himself by an inadequate grasp of the field. There are some *common pigeonholes into which licensors can put their licensing program.* Each mistake would reveal that the company has poorly defined the program.

The first error goes something like this: "Since we want the licensing effort to extend our brand imagery, it follows that it should be part of brand/product management rather than a separate department." This is wrong because licensing should be linked directly, as explained earlier, to the overall corporate strategy, of which brands and brand imagery are a part—an integral part, but a part.

Related to the first pigeonhole is another: "Licenses are essentially contracts; lawyers help govern the association of licensor and licensee in the early stages; therefore, put licensing under the legal department." Although there needs to be strong legal support in a licensing program, to limit its effectiveness by putting licensing under the legal staff would be a grave misjudgment. The skills that lawyers possess have nothing to do with making a licensing effort tick. They're paid to safeguard, not to create and market.

A little more subtle licensing heresy is to hold that licensing belongs with the new product development department. While it's true that licensing involves new products, that's hardly a full definition. Licensing generally involves *someone else's product,* or *even an image without a product* (there's no Mickey Mantle product for sale in his "Mickey's" restaurant, for example). Licensing extends far beyond new product develoment.

Finally, some licensors think they can shove the whole program off on the advertising agency. While the agency will doubtless generate some fresh ideas, it's a conflict of interest for the agency to run a licensor's licensing program. The agency is paid to find creative ways to market a product. Generally, when an agency offers to do licensing as well as handle advertising for the core product, they offer a discount on their percentage for product advertising. So they are left with an incentive to spend more time and effort on the licensing program to make up the difference in lost income. Worse, in some cases, they do ad campaigns to sell the licensed product for the revenue it brings them—not for the sake of advancing the core product. Giving the ad agency the licensing program can easily result in a warping of the proper view and function of the program.

A second pitfall for licensing managers is in *execution before strategy.* No matter how exciting a given licensing venture looks, no matter what its potential, prudence demands that you map out a strategy first, then develop your marketing tactics, and only thereafter do you implement. Many licensing programs do the execution first, and quickly derail because there is no end or direction beyond marketing a given item or series of related products. Inevitably, the effort peters out, leaving a bad taste in the mouths of company decision makers. If they were ill-disposed to licensing before the effort, they become unalterably opposed to the whole idea of licensing afterwards. Wendy's "Where's the Beef" licensing effort is a classic example of execution before strategy. When the ad campaign—which was terrific—ended, so did the licensing program.

A final pitfall is *licensing mania*—the infatuation with any licensing idea presented to you. Generally, it's the fetching notion of all that free exposure that blinds a potential licensor in this case. But we've seen that the quickest way to destroy a licensing program and cheapen the company image is to license your trademark or brand indiscriminately. It's no excuse to say that, after all, the trademark or brand is so popular that the consumer demands it. In fact, any licensing program that grabs every opportunity offered it by every licensee who comes along is destined to collapse. It's all but a mathematical certainty that the majority of concepts that will be broached to you by potential licensees will not live up to your standards. Nor will many of the licensees themselves. This would certainly be true of a noted ice cream bar company that licensed its products to different dairies across the country. It would be hard to implement strict quality control standards in such a variety of licensee plants. As a result, the product would vary in taste, depending on the area of the country and its manufacturer. This in turn would hurt sales, which would dampen licensee interest. You can write the rest of the story.

Not to be overlooked by the licensing administrator is the obligation to plow back licensing profits—a portion of them—into the program. A fixed percentage of the royalties should be set aside to cultivate licensee support as well as to research and develop further ventures. The natural tendency is to see licensing revenue as "found money" (true)—and run out and spend it. Examples of those who spend some of that found money wisely: Disney and Major League Baseball.

Growth and How to Handle It

In a smoothly running licensing program, new venture opportunities will constantly arise (via licensee proposals or through your own research). But one never stokes the boiler without monitoring the gauges as well, and in the licensing effort, all ventures must be checked against the company's overall objectives for a brand or product. Too, the licensee must prove to the licensor's satisfaction that he or she has the staying power and can be effective for the duration of the venture.

The licensing administrator must also build a structure that can handle growth. As a licensing department's objectives and programs are carried out, its makeup will change. This may mean additional people at all levels, including management; more controls and defined procedures, added support elements for the licensees, more communication with more licensees.

There are growth licensees you'll deal with, and there are one-timers. A *growth licensee* is a company that not only has a good idea for today, but has an internal structure to create and execute good ideas for the future. When evaluating a licensee, it must be determined whether this licensee has growth potential or is merely banking on you/the licensed product for easy salvation; these last are the *one-timers*. When a company is using your trademark to save its own hide, you may be running the risk of loading your valuable possession onto something headed for the glue factory. Best to deal with companies that are using yours to help their own healthy businesses grow.

Moreover, the licensor must determine where this trademark fits into the licensee's overall business plans. It isn't necessarily good that a licensee makes your licensed product its top priority. In most cases, in fact, this should give you pause, because it may mean that yours is the licensee's only licensed property, which in turn might well mean that the company is too small or inexperienced to do the job well (or to have staying power; new and small businesses fold at a high rate). Having said that, one must admit that once in a while an entrepreneurial licensee comes along who makes you the focus of his business, and you rocket to the top of the sales charts. Still, this is different from a licensee whose existing business has been in a period of prolonged decline and is looking for a property to save it.

Should your licensee give you an exclusive in your product category? That all depends. Apparel, footwear, toys—these are ultra-competitive categories where a licensee generally *can't* give an exclusive. Volume can be critical for them. Also, if the licensor is going into a product category where the only thing differentiating that product from the competition's is the brand name or logo (categories such as T-shirts, bedsheets, and lighters) then the licensor can't expect the licensee to give an exclusive. When the licensee goes to a retailer in cases like

• **Cap'n Crunch Toy Chest—marketed for a time by a licensee, American Toy & Furniture Company, Inc.—extended the brand image into a logical new area.** (Courtesy American Toy & Furniture Company, Inc.)

these, he or she needs a whole line of goods to offer. Exclusivity should be asked for, however, if the licensor has both a trademark *and* a concept that is so unique it more or less "earns" an exclusive. Even here, of course, the licensee must weigh the value to its own business of the trademark/concept proposed.

It is helpful to look on your licensees the way an investor looks on a portfolio of investments. You must manage the licensee portfolio. You've taken a good deal of your company's wealth—its good name and trademarks—and invested it with a select group of companies. These companies must be tracked like stocks, evaluated continuously. You'll quickly find which of them is best and most reliable, worthy of further investment.

Appendix D contains Major League Baseball Properties' "Prospective Licensee Information Form." Every would-be licensee for Major League Baseball must fill the form out and face the scrutiny it implies. The form contains all the elements a licensor needs to evaluate a potential licensee, and we reprint it, in its entirety, with the kind permission of Major League Baseball Properties. It's as thorough as anything like it in the licensing industry, and will prove as valuable for licensees to study as it will for licensors.

CHAPTER 5

LICENSING THE "U.S.A."

How do you launch a real licensing program? Let's take a fictional client, the United States government (U.S.A.), and go step by step through the initial stages of a licensing effort. We've chosen the U.S.A. because it has a wealth of equity, as you'll soon see, that has gone untapped. The client obviously has a big problem: it spends more money than it has. The CEO has authorized a broad array of income-producing steps, including exploring the possibility of licensing some of the U.S.A.'s properties.

Actually we will take you through all the stages of the business plan, but when illustrating each stage, the focus will be mostly on the start-up phase. That is the trickiest and most complicated.

The major elements in the U.S.A.'s licensing program plan are:

- Corporate strategic objectives/charter.
- Analysis of brand equities, complete with trademark review.
- Exploring areas of opportunity for brand extension.
- Brand extension: development of specific concepts.
- Evaluating the concepts.
- Setting up the licensing administration department.
- Product and licensee development.
- Market development.
- Pull-through programs.

Corporate Strategic Objectives/Charter

This licensing program is designed to extend the U.S.A.'s trademarks for profit, and also to protect assets that have long been ignored. The program is further intended to improve the citizens' view of their nation and to educate Americans via affordable, quality products. Given the problems of debt and increased competition from Japan, Inc., and others, the need is urgent. (Notice that the charter and objectives cover three areas: business, image, and promotional.)

Analysis of Brand Equities and Trademark Review

What does the government own that is marketable? A list of properties and trademarks turns up a wealth of things—and a legal review is undertaken to make doubly sure the U.S.A. does own (and has *protected*) the properties we think could conceivably yield licensing concepts. For the sake of this exercise, the legal review checks out. In meetings with the top government executives, the cabinet secretaries, these U.S.A. properties (broad categories, that is) were deemed to have the most potential:

- Government logos and seals, including things like the FBI and, of course, the Presidential seal.
- The White House, certain federal office buildings, monuments, state parks, and national historic landmarks.
- The Postal Service's stamp archives.
- NASA and the space program.
- The armed services, particularly weaponry but also nostalgia items such as old planes and uniforms.
- The Smithsonian Institution and other museums.

After deciding which are the most attractive trademarks and properties within each of the above groupings and evaluating which ones would most appeal to potential licensees, a first round of focus group research is done in the next phase.

Exploring Areas of Opportunity for Brand Extension

The consumers in focus groups should be probed to discover what level of appeal each of the property categories has, and what image they have of particular properties. What products and services come to their minds when property X or Y is presented to them? Let's assume that after this first round, we ascertain that our focus should be on the following properties: the White House and federal buildings, parks and historic landmarks, and monuments. And we further deduced that the following product and service categories constitute our "areas of licensing opportunity":

- Entertainment.
- Food.
- Clothing and apparel.
- Collectibles.
- Toys and games.
- Educational tools.
- Stationery.

Brand Extension: Development of Specific Concepts

We take these results back to the government and discuss them in a "concept generation session." We learn which areas the government is particularly interested in exploiting; for example, the secretary of the interior (let's assume that he's our new boss, a kind of group vice president, because all the properties fall under his authority) wants to educate Americans about our national parks. The secretary is also interested in enlarging the budget. With the top Interior Department people (from all the subdivisions of that bureaucracy) we generate dozens of product and service concepts, some of them borrowed from focus group participants, by the way. In the process, potential licensees are inevitably discussed as well. And at the same time the concept generation meetings take place—over a period of two or three weeks, let's say—the company should begin to look seriously at staffing a licensing department and finding an administrator. Indeed, hiring for the department could already have taken place, and will have to, in short order.

As for the concepts generated in the sessions, let's list them by "area of opportunity":

Entertainment

White House Inns—franchise hotels, exact replicas of 1600 Pennsylvania Ave.

Food

Yellowstone Soup—the finest ingredients.
White House brand foods—the kind traditionally served to the presidents.
Grand Canyon cake.

Yellowstone quick-eat food for campers.

Air Force One snacks.

Mt. Rushmore candy bars—"a monumental taste."

Old Faithful mineral water—"it's not available just anywhere."

Yellowstone mud packs.

Grand Canyon sundaes.

White House cookbooks.

Yellowstone Redwoods—hearty snack chips "like nothing you've ever seen before."

Fort Knox candy bar—"24 karats: the richest candy bar in the world."

Toys and Games

Yellowstone stuffed animals.

Premiums for Cracker Jacks, cereals, etc.: miniature monuments.

Presidential trains.

White House doll house.

"Building Our Nation's Capital"—models of monuments and buildings.

Puzzles of monuments, buildings, parks (e.g., air views)

Stationery

Vietnam Memorial letterhead for veterans and their families only.

"God Bless America" Christmas cards.

Educational Videos

White House videos—all about the presidents.

National Park stories.

From the Nation's Archives—a series based on the massive amount of photos and films from White House and congressional, as well as Smithsonian, sources.

Collectibles

Ceramic plates—limited edition replicas of White House china (from various administrations).

Official presidential portraits—copies of the White House originals.

Pewter figurines—monuments such as the Iwo Jima Memorial, the Gateway Arch.

"Our Great Heritage" collector card series—presidents, legislators, judges of note.

Clothing, Apparel, Accessories

Yellowstone Stores (and mail-order catalog)—outerwear, camping equipment.

Air Force One executive luggage—"for the President, and you"

Air Force One accessories—sunglasses, aviator jackets.

Miscellaneous

Rose Garden roses

"State of the Union" wallpaper—commemorating great events.

"State of the Union" home furnishings.

The Presidential "Hotline"—communications systems.

Book: "In Case You're Invited to the White House: Etiquette for Citizens from All Walks of Life."

"Secret Service" Electronics (SS Electronics)—consumer high-tech electronics.

Note that actual concept-generation sessions should produce double this number of product ideas.

Evaluating the Concepts

Concurrent with this phase, the licensing department is being formed, and the people lined up to staff it should be participating in the second round of focus groups (as they have, if they've been picked for the staff, in the first round). In this round, all the concepts that have been generated are taken to consumers for their reaction. If possible, prototype samples of some of the proposed products, or their packaging or designs, should be presented to consumers. Which ones strike a chord; which seem most interesting? Obviously, those would go the top of the list.

Let's assume, for the sake of simplicity, that our evaluating has led us to focus all our efforts on five concepts (as many as a dozen *could* have been chosen):

1. Fort Knox candy bar.
2. Old Faithful mineral water.
3. White House Inns.
4. Official presidential portraits.
5. SS Electronics.

The Remaining Elements of the Licensing Plan

Let's further assume that the next task, *setting up a licensing administration department,* has been completed according to the prescriptions in the earlier chapter. We'll now move into the last three elements of our licensing plan: product and licensee development, market development, and "pull-through" programs (this last really being a function of market development). We will refer arbitrarily to any one of the five finalists above to illustrate our points, but the Fort Knox candy bar will be a favorite. Since the final three elements are intertwined, we'll take them as one and break down the tasks involved, using the following outline developed by my colleagues at Conposit:

1. Product design.
2. Product plan.
3. Distribution/pricing plan.
4. Promotional and advertising strategy.
5. Trademark adaptation/graphics.
6. Licensee/manufacturer development.
7. Retail development.
8. Pull-through.

1. Product Design.   A detailed concept statement about the product and the trademark to be used is provided to the licensee. The concept statement briefly outlines why the product will work, what exactly it is, and why it's being marketed. For the Fort Knox candy bar, we might say the following: "This is to be marketed as the richest and most expensive candy bar in the country. At this level of the candy market, some room exists to compete successfully, and with the clout of the licensor, not to mention its help with distribution and promotion, quick success is expected." As for package design, we'll opt for a double gold foil wrapper, embossed with a Fort Knox–like insignia.

2. Product Plan.   We've already decided to bring the Fort Knox bar out as a licensed product, but in many cases, a potential licensor may wonder whether the product should be self-manufactured by contracting it out and keeping ownership to itself, or perhaps making it a joint venture proposition. Sometimes, a product looks just too profitable to let go. A licensor may deem it both profitable and so close to its own product line that it would be better to keep the concept.

3. Distribution/Pricing Plan.   While the broad outline of this plan should be thought out by the licensor before approaching any licensee, the final plan in all its details should await discussions with the licensee. Example: our fictional "Secret Service" Electronics. We think it's upscale, so we want distribution to be limited to stores such as Sharper Image and high-fashion department stores, rather than the K marts and Penneys of the industry. Pricing is related to this. Higher prices dictate different distribution, to a large extent.

4. Promotional and Advertising Strategy.   We're merging two related but distinct areas. How best to let the world know about the new Fort Knox candy bar? Promotions have been described in an earlier chapter, but let's apply some of those ideas to this product and the licensor's promotional capabilities. With the Interior Department involved, the first thing to do is call a press conference (which many other licensors can also do). The Fort Knox candy bar is to be promoted like the issue of a new gold coin. All government facilities will carry it, of course. And all federally produced brochures will promote the "Bar of Bars" as well. The candy bar will be promoted as though it were a news event. The interior secretary will bring along the agriculture secretary—or better yet, hold a separate press conference the following month—to announce that the Fort Knox chocolate bar will be extended into another category: chocolate milk. No more paying dairy farmers to dump "excess" milk!

5. Trademark Adaptation/Graphics.   The licensor should provide the licensee with guidelines, if not actual ideas, for artistic adaptation of the trademarks to be used in licensing. A graphics package that precisely depicts each logo should be developed. Representatives from Fort Knox, Yellowstone National Park, and the Secret Service, for example, should supply their licensee with exact reproductions of their logos, along with whatever restrictions they deem appropriate regarding artistic freedom. Graphic artists are creative, but the more creative an artist is, the more the artist needs to be told of any parameters beyond which it's not permissible to go. For example, the color of Yellowstone's logo shouldn't be changed to red and black from yellow and green, or reshaped so that it is hard to recognize.

5. Licensee/Manufacturer Development.   The conventional choice for a big licensor like the U.S.A. would be a major candy manufacturer for the Fort Knox candy bar. (We've ruled out, by the way, contract development. The U.S.A. needs a licensee to make this concept fly.) But picking a smaller licensee is by no means to be ruled out. Smaller companies often operate more efficiently for a bigger partner, in part because they have so much to gain from the relationship.

7. Retail Development. The "given" outlets for Fort Knox candy: military bases, federally run tourist spots, and national parks and monuments, not to mention federal office buildings. New outlets we'd need to develop: the major upscale retailers. Here's a product that's absolutely original and provides real news for their customers.

8. Pull-Through Program. The candy wrappers themselves should contain a form to be saved and filled out. After a certain number is accumulated, the buyer would send in for a certificate entitling him or her—and the family—to 50 percent off the cost of a ticket to any federally run tourist site in the United States. In this way, a large and well-defined mailing list would be built that could be rented for profit and perhaps tested with a mail-order catalog containing other U.S.A. company licensed items.

Thus is our licensing program for the U.S.A. launched.

Chapter 6

THE REWARDS OF
GOOD LICENSING

INCREASING BUSINESS PRODUCTIVITY

By employing a business tool called licensing, you will engage in a practice that has been misunderstood, or only partly understood, for as long as it's been around. Licensing isn't new. In fact, it's an organic outgrowth of sound business marketing and management. But its value as a distinct and vital part of any company is only now being recognized—by some, anyway.

Many companies regard licensing as a "something for nothing" proposition, and therefore it is suspect. A brand new avenue on which to compete—at little or no financial cost? It seems too good to be true. Several potential licensors have spurned millions of dollars worth of licensing opportunities because of an almost philosophical belief: nothing good comes cheap. Lots of things come cheap, actually—but let us turn the equation around: All the consumer goodwill and confidence that companies have "paid for" over the years amount to "interest" that has never been invested or tapped in any way—if they haven't licensed themselves. Licensing takes all that accrued interest out from under the mattress and spends it to buy new consumers or to keep happy the ones your company already has. They will have a deeper loyalty. All that is a lot for something, not something for nothing.

Another way that licensing helps to increase business productivity is by creating marketing efficiences. Licensing and efficiency go hand in hand. Using the marketing assets of the company, the licensor gets more out of them than their evident value.

• **Even "colorless" companies such as Rust-Oleum Corporation can employ licensing. The familiar Rust-Oleum^{sm} logo will now appear on certain quality tool sheds and swing sets.** (Courtesy Equity Management, Inc., of Chicago.)

MINIMIZING NEW VENTURE RISK

In the last decade or so, new product/new business development costs have soared as the price of entry has risen. The price of failure has gone up alongside. Licensing gives a licensor the opportunity to achieve market penetration without capital investment. New ventures can be attempted without investing great amounts of company resources and diverting expertise (both of which are essential when you otherwise launch new products by themselves). It is easier for a snack company, for example, to license its well-known logo than to market a new kind of product, all by itself, in a related but new category. Moreover, a licensing venture can be launched much faster than a new product venture.

Many companies abandon potential new businesses because they think they don't have the expertise, time, or resources to experiment. Licensing offers them a bridge to new markets without taking a "new product" type of risk.

Licensing also enables a company to enter industries that it would otherwise be suicidal to try to reach. Through a licensee, a licensor can not only enter a completely new industry and reap the benefits via royalties, but it can acquire expertise in the new industry as well. Licensees offer a great deal of information to licensors, who, as their business partners, are privy to marketing secrets closed to most others.

• Over 1 billion Archie milk cartons have been distributed through a licensing arrangement. The benefit to Archie Comics sales should be obvious, even though in this case Archie Comics collects no royalties. (Courtesy Archie Comic Publications, Inc.)

• Profitable: Collegiate licensing, which has added millions to the coffers of certain institutions of higher learning. (Courtesy Joy Insignia, Inc., Deerfield Beach, Florida.)

The Exposure Factor

What advertising value does a licensed product in the promotional licensing category have? Here's an admittedly unscientific way to measure that. Let's take a T-shirt with a consumer products company's brand on it. It costs $12 retail, and 100,000 people buy it. 100,000 consumers, in other words, are saying that the trademark is *worth* that much to them. A table measuring exposure value might look something like this:

Factors

Licensed item: T-shirt
Wholesale price: $6
Retail price: $12
Number of units sold: 100,000
Product life: 3 years
Royalty rate for licensor: 7 percent of *wholesale* price

The Calculation

Number of units sold × Retail price = Advertising/exposure dollars
100,000 × $12 = $1,200,000 first-year exposure factor
Second-year exposure factor = $799,000 (66 percent of first year)
Third-year exposure factor = $399,600 (33 percent of first year)
Total exposure factor: $2,398,800
Plus royalty: $42,000 (7 percent of the wholesale price)

Let's assume at least 500 people see each T-shirt in its three-year life span. That's 50 million people who see the licensor's trademark, though of course not 50 million different people. Still, a company would have to pay at least hundreds of thousands to buy that kind of exposure any other way. But with licensing, people pay the company.

STRENGTHENING THE CORE BUSINESS AND COMPANY ASSETS

Apart from the royalties licensing brings to the licensor, it extends the core brand's image in a quality way, thus generating exposure for the brand to new consumer bases. Used properly in conjunction with an advertising campaign, licensing multiplies the value of the ad budget; that is, the ad itself can generate interest not only in the core product, but in the licensed product as well. In addition, on the retail level, the exposure generated by licensed items comes at no cost. If the same exposure were to be purchased via advertising or promotion dollars, the sum required would be considerable. With licensing it is quite the opposite—the licensor is getting *paid* (via royalties) for advertising its brand. Expansion of absolute marketing exposure through licensing has never been quantified, but for every Coke rugby shirt out there lasting three to five years, if thousands of people see it, that's a great deal of advertising and money saved.

TRADEMARK/BRAND PROTECTION AND CONTROL

Licensing your trademark is one of the prime ways to legally protect it both in its core category and in other, secondary product categories into which you wish to expand. Provided the licensor can show that it has taken steps to control the trademark/logo use in a product category *and* to protect it generally, its legal claim is solid. This can translate into untold amounts of money later on in the life of a company. One beverage maker, for example, has established a brand name, "Jaguar," in an ancillary product category. One of its competitors wanted that name for a new brand of its own, only to find the claim was solid. The trademark would have had to be purchased from its competitor. For Anheuser-Busch, the slogan "This Bud's for You" was lost to a shrewd licensor, The Florists Association of Greater Cleveland, which established worldwide licensing rights to that phrase for its own product category because Anheuser-Busch hadn't established trademark protection of it across the board. (The appearance of its ad slogan in another product category can't hurt it, though it would have been far preferable if Anheuser-Busch itself could collect the royalties.)

• A familiar line that was unprotected in a specific product category is used to best advantage by a relatively unknown organization, The Florists Association of Greater Cleveland, Inc. Here is their ad announcing their trademark's availability for licensing.
(Courtesy Harry Gard Shaffer, Jr./The Florists Association of Greater Cleveland, Inc.)

The potential for losing trademark protection in the international arena is great. Several big corporations have lost the use of some of their American brand names in international markets because they hadn't registered their marks in those markets. Without getting into the intricacies of international law, suffice it to say that establishing trademark use in *some* category internationally is better than none at all. Licensing could be the avenue for this, too.

Licensing may also enable the licensor to protect a trademark for later, more extensive use. If you are a small company and you have a great trademark for a product, but lack the product itself, you can gain great leverage by protecting the trademark through a licensed item, and perhaps later, selling it. If you have a large company, you may well be aware how difficult it is to find good trademarks. If you've got one but lack a product to match it, don't let it get away. Through a licensing program, try to put a claim on that trademark.

In May of 1988, *Fortune* magazine devoted an issue to innovators in business. Though licensing wasn't its focus, we found the cover story fascinating. It outlined the very point we want to leave with you:

One way or another, thousands of product lines in every type of industry are being transformed. Innovating—creating new products, new services, new ways of turning out goods more cheaply—has become the most urgent concern of corporations everywhere. That is partly because restructuring has left many companies with a few core businesses that are solid but slow growing. Innovation is their best bet for revving things up. . . . Innovation is this year's hot word . . . and the subject of several new management advice books.

No matter what the climate for business, the fact is that once a company reaches a certain level of success, growth becomes increasingly difficult. Stagnation is uncomfortable, and decline, of course, unthinkable. Licensing could well be an answer. Indeed, a *real* licensing program, one that lasts and is tended to carefully, can be like life insurance for the licensor. It gives the target consumer more reasons to buy from you, more reasons to be loyal to your company or brand.

Loyalty to a brand is the consumer's way of reducing risk, of justifying the limiting of his or her choices. Most people are averse to risk and want to become confident in particular brands. Once they are loyal, they should be cultivated, their loyalty reinforced and capitalized on. Licensors who are able to offer additional products to such consumers make it harder for them to abandon their core brand. And *that* factor could be crucial to your company in a business downturn or recession.

APPENDIX A

MERCHANDISING LICENSE AGREEMENT, ANNOTATED

Probably the foremost licensing legal experts in the country, Gregory J. Battersby and Charles W. Grimes form the law firm of Grimes & Battersby, have written two textbooks on licensing, *The Law of Merchandising and Character Licensing* and *Licensing Law Handbook,* both published by Clark Boardman. With their permission and with the permission of *The Merchandising Reporter* journal (where this licensing contract has appeared) we reprint it in full, complete with their explanatory notes.*

PROVISION	COMMENTARY
AGREEMENT	
THIS AGREEMENT is made this 1st day of May, 1987 by and between Pennfair Productions, Inc., a New York corporation with offices at 242 Park Avenue, New York, New York 10000 (the "Licensor") and Bestbilt Products, Inc., a Mississippi corporation with offices at 123 Main Street, Bridgehampton, MS 55555 (the "Licensee").	This paragraph sets the stage by identifying the licensor and licensee and establishes the effective date of the agreement.
WITNESSETH	
WHEREAS, the Licensor is the owner of a copyrighted character described and/or illustrated in Schedule A attached hereto (the "Property") and of the Trademark(s) listed in Schedule A attached hereto (the "Trademarks");	This paragraph defines the Licensed Property and Trademark as identified in the attached Schedule A.[1]

---

* *The Merchandising Reporter,* Pennfair Communications Inc., P.O. Box 1311, Stamford, Conn. 06904, $125 per year.

[1] [Author's note: "Schedule A," not presented here, simply contains all the details and particulars that vary from case to case.]

PROVISION	COMMENTARY
WHEREAS, the Licensee desires to use the Property and/or the Trademarks on or in association with the manufacture, offering for sale, sale, advertising, promotion, and distribution of certain products identified in Schedule A attached hereto (the "Licensed Products") in the countries identified in Schedule A attached hereto (the "Licensed Territory"); and	The Licensed Products and Licensed Territory are defined per their identification in Schedule A.
WHEREAS, the Licensor is willing to grant the Licensee the right to use the Property and/or the Trademarks on the Licensed Products in the Licensed Territory in accordance with the terms and conditions recited herein.	
NOW, THEREFORE, in consideration of the mutual promises, covenants and conditions herein contained, it is hereby agreed as follows:	

1. *GRANT*
   (a) The Licensor hereby grants to the Licensee an exclusive, nontransferable, non-assignable license, without the right to grant sublicenses, to use the Property solely on and/or in association with the manufacture, offering for sale, sale, advertising, promotion, shipment and distribution of the Licensed Products solely within the Licensed Territory.

   Commentary: This is the operative exclusive license grant to use the Property. It is non-transferable and prevents the granting of sub-licenses.

   (b) The Licensor hereby further grants to the Licensee an exclusive, non-transferable, non-assignable license, without the right to grant sublicenses, to use the Trademarks solely on and/or in association with the manufacture, offering for sale, sale, advertising, promotion, shipment and distribution of the Licensed Products and solely within the Licensed Territory.

   Commentary: This is the operative exclusive license grant to use the Trademark on Licensed Products and on Promotional and Advertising Material with no right to transfer the rights or grant sub-licenses.

2. *TERM*
   This Agreement shall commence and be effective upon execution of this Agreement

   Commentary: By reference to Schedule A, this establishes when

PROVISION	COMMENTARY

by both parties (the "Effective Date") and shall run from the Effective Date hereof for the Term recited in Schedule A attached hereto (the "Term") unless sooner terminated pursuant to a provision of this Agreement.

the Agreement commences and ends.

3. *ROYALTY PROVISIONS*

    (a) Licensee agrees to pay the Licensor the Royalty recited in Schedule A attached hereto based on Licensee's Net Sales of the Licensed Products (the "Actual Royalty").

By reference to Schedule A, this defines the royalty rate.

    (b) Actual Royalty payments shall be made by the Licensee to the Licensor on all Licensed Products sold, shipped and/or distributed by the Licensee, even if not billed (such as in the case of introductory offers, samples, promotions and the like and sales, shipments and/or distributions to individuals and/or companies which are affiliated or associated with and/or subsidiaries of Licensee), based upon the Licensee's usual net sales price for such Licensed Products sold to third parties in the course of the Licensee's normal distribution, shipment and sales activities.

This provision defines the types of transactions for which a royalty is due.

    (c) Where the billed price for any Licensed Products is less than the usual net sales price for such Licensed Products sold to third parties in the course of the Licensee's normal distribution, shipment and sales activities, the Actual Royalty payment shall be based upon the Licensee's usual net sales price.

This provision provides that a full royalty shall be paid for distressed sales.

    (d) For the Term of this Agreement, the Licensee agrees to pay the Licensor a non-refundable, "Minimum Royalty" in the amount recited in Schedule A attached hereto. Of the Minimum Royalty, the Licensee agrees to pay to the Licensor a non-refundable Advance

The Minimum Royalty and Advances identified in Schedule A are recited. It specifically provides that the actual royalty payments will be credited against the Minimum Royalty.

PROVISION	COMMENTARY

against Royalties ("Advance") in the amount recited in Schedule A which is due and payable upon execution of this Agreement. Actual Royalty payments based on Net sales made during the Term of this Agreement shall be credited against the Minimum Royalty due for the Term in which such Net sales were made.

(e) "Net Sales" shall mean gross sales less quantity discounts and returns actually credited. No deductions shall be made for cash or other discounts, for commissions, for uncollectable accounts, or for taxes, fees, assessments, impositions, payments or expenses of any kind.

    A definition is provided for "Net Sales." This provision should be reviewed by the Licensor's accountants.

(f) In addition to all amounts payable to Licensor, Licensee shall pay the Licensor a Promotional Fee in the amount recited in Schedule A, which amount shall be payable monthly. Licensor agrees to match such amount dollar for dollar and to expend the total sum for Licensor advertising or promotional activities.

    If a promotional fee is required, it would be recited in Schedule A.

4. *STATEMENTS AND PAYMENTS*

(a) The Licensee shall provide the Licensor, within thirty (30) days after the end of each calendar quarter (the "Royalty Period"), a complete and accurate statement of its Net Sales of Licensed Products for the Royalty Period in conformance with the sample statement attached hereto as Schedule B. Said statement is to be certified as accurate by the Licensee and to include information as to the number, description and gross selling price of the Licensed Products shipped, distributed and/or sold by the Licensee during the

    This provision defines the royalty period and the type of statements which must be submitted to the licensor. The statement should be certified by an officer of the licensee.

PROVISION	COMMENTARY

preceding Royalty Period, information as to discounts given and returns actually credited and any other further information as the Licensor may from time to time request. Such statements shall be furnished to the Licensor whether or not any Licensed Products have been shipped, distributed and/or sold and whether or not Actual Royalties have been earned during the preceding Royalty Period.

(b) The amount shown in the Licensee's quarterly statements as being due the Licensor shall be paid simultaneously with the submission of such statements. In no event shall the amount credited for quantity discounts and returns during any Royalty Period exceed the Licensee's Royalty obligation for such Royalty Period or be used as a credit against past or future Royalty obligations of the Licensee.

Payments are to be made simultaneously with the submission of the quarterly statements. Under no circumstances should there be a negative cash flow in which the Licensor is obligated to return money to the Licensee.

(c) The Licensee's quarterly statements and all amounts payable to the Licensor by the Licensee shall be submitted to the address stated above, attention: Chief Financial Officer.

(d) The receipt and/or acceptance by the Licensor of any of the statements furnished or Royalties paid hereunder to the Licensor (or the cashing of any Royalty checks paid hereunder) shall not preclude the Licensor from questioning the correctness thereof at any time and, in the event that any inconsistencies or mistakes are discovered in such statements or payments, they shall immediately be rectified by the Licensee and the appropriate payment shall be made by the Licensee.

The cashing of a royalty check by the Licensor should not constitute a waiver to prevent it from being able to subsequentially challenge the correctness thereof.

PROVISION	COMMENTARY
(e) All payments made hereunder shall be in United States currency drawn on a United States bank, unless otherwise specifically agreed upon by the parties.	This is particularly relevant with regard to foreign Licensees. It requires that all payments be made in U.S. currency drawn on a U.S. bank. In this manner, the Licensor is not obligated for bank collection fees for processing foreign checks.
(f) Time is of the essence with respect to all payments to be made hereunder by the Licensee. Interest at a rate of one and one-half percent (1½%) per month shall accrue on any amount due the Licensor hereunder from and after the date upon which the payment is due until the date of receipt of payment.	This is a standard "time is of the essence" provision with interest accruing for late payments.

5. *AUDIT*

(a) The Licensee agrees to keep accurate books of account and records at its principal place of business covering all transactions relating to the License being granted herein. The Licensor and its duly authorized representatives shall have the right, at all reasonable hours of the day, to audit the Licensee's books of account and records and all other documents and material in the possession or under the control of the Licensee with respect to the subject matter and the terms of this Agreement and to make copies and extracts thereof. In the event that any such audit reveals an underpayment by the Licensee, the Licensee shall immediately remit payment to the Licensor in the amount of such underpayment plus interest calculated at the rate of one and one-half percent (1½%) per month calculated from the date such payment(s) were	The audit provision is a relatively standard audit provision which should be reviewed with the auditors the Licensor plans to use for auditing Licensees. It provides that the Licensor has a right to audit under reasonable terms. In the event that the audit reveals an underpayment in excess of $500, the Licensee is obligated to pay for the cost of the audit.

PROVISION	COMMENTARY

actually due until the date when such payment is, in fact, actually made. Further, in the event that any such underpayment is greater than $500 for any Royalty Period, the Licensee shall reimburse the Licensor for the costs and expenses of such audit including, but not limited to, reasonable attorneys' fees incurred in connection therewith.

(b) Upon demand by the Licensor, but not more than once each year, the Licensee shall, at its own cost, furnish the Licensor with a detailed statement, prepared by an independent certified public accountant of the Licensee's choice and acceptable to the Licensor, setting forth the number of Licensed Products manufactured during the time period extending from the later of the Effective Date of this Agreement or the date of any previous statement up to and including the date of the statement and also setting forth the pricing information for all Licensed Products (including the number and description of the Licensed Products) shipped, distributed and/or sold by the Licensee during the aforementioned time period.

In many instances the Licensor will want a certified statement prepared by an outside auditor with regard to actual sales of Licensed Products. Oftentimes, the Licensee will require that the Licensor bear the cost for such an audit.

(c) All books of account and records of the Licensee covering all transactions relating to the License shall be retained by the Licensee for at least two (2) years after the expiration or termination of this Agreement for possible inspection by the Licensor.

One problem frequently encountered is destruction of records. This provision requires that the Licensee keep all books and records for at least two years after expiration of the agreement.

6. *QUALITY, NOTICES, APPROVALS, AND SAMPLES*

(a) The quality of the Licensed Products as well as the quality of all promotional, advertising and packaging material which includes the Property and/or the

The quality control provision is the heart of any merchandising license agreement and is required

PROVISION	COMMENTARY
Trademarks (the "Promotional and Packaging Material") shall be at least as high as the best quality of similar products and promotional, advertising and packaging material presently shipped, distributed, sold and/or used by the Licensee in the Licensed Territory and shall be in full conformance with all applicable laws and regulations.	when a trademark is being licensed.
(b) The Licensee may not manufacture, use, offer for sale, sell, advertise, promote, ship and/or distribute any Licensed Products nor any Promotional and Packaging Material relating to the Licensed Products until it has received written approval of same in the manner provided herein from the Licensor. Such approval may be granted or withheld as the Licensor, in its sole discretion, may determine. Should the Licensor fail to approve in writing any of the submissions furnished it by the Licensee within fourteen (14) days from the date of submission thereof, such failure shall be considered to be a disapproval thereof.	This provides that the Licensee cannot manufacture or sell Licensed Products without prior approval by the Licensor. A portion frequently negotiated is the affect of the Licensor's failure to approve within the requisite time and whether such failure to approve should constitute approval or disapproval.
(c) Before commencing or authorizing third parties to commence the design or development of Licensed Products or of Promotional and Packaging Material which have not been previously approved in writing by the Licensor, the Licensee shall submit at its own cost to the Licensor, for approval, a description of the concept of the same, including full information on the nature and function of the proposed item and a general description of how the Property and/or the Trademarks and other material will be used thereon. The Licensee shall next submit at its own cost to	This paragraph recites the basic submission requirements for Licensor approval. It must be understood that it is in the Licensee's best interest to obtain product approval at as early a date as possible to avoid scrapping or destroying already manufactured products

PROVISION	COMMENTARY
the Licensor, for approval, complete layouts and descriptions of the proposed Licensed Products and/or Promotional and Packaging Material showing exactly how and where the Property and the Trademarks and all other artwork and wording will be used. Thereafter, the Licensee shall submit, at its own cost, to the Licensor for approval, pre-production models or prototype samples of the proposed Licensed Products and/or Promotional and Packaging Material. Finally, the Licensee shall submit, at its own cost, to the Licensor for approval, actual production samples of the proposed Licensed Products and/or Promotional and Packaging Material (the "Production Samples"). The Licensee shall not proceed beyond any of the above stages where approval is required without first securing the prior express written approval of the Licensor.	
(d) The Licensee agrees that all Licensed Products and all Promotional and Packaging Material shall contain appropriate legends, markings and/or notices as required from time to time by the Licensor, to give appropriate notice to the consuming public of the Licensor's right, title and interest thereto. The Licensee agrees that, unless otherwise expressly approved in writing by the Licensor, each usage of the Trademarks shall be followed by the Licensor, each usage of the Trademarks shall be followed by either the TM or the Circle R Trademark Notice symbol, as appropriate, and initially the following legends shall appear at least once on each Licensed Product and on each	This is a standard copyright and trademark provision.

PROVISION	COMMENTARY

piece of Promotional and Packaging Material:
 	
Copr. or™ Pennfair Productions, Inc., 1987
    All Rights Reserved
™ and ® Desginate Trademarks of Pennfair
    Productions, Inc.
(e) The Licensee shall use no other markings, legends and/or notices on or in association with the Licensed Products or on or in association with the Promotional and Packaging Material other than the above specified legend and such other markings, legends and/or notices as may from time to time be specified by the Licensor, without first obtaining the Licensor's prior express written approval.
	This paragraph puts the teeth in the previous paragraph and requires that the Licensee use no other markings or legal notices other than as required by the Licensor.

(f) Upon commencement of manufacture, shipment and distribution of the Licensed Products and/or Promotional and Packaging Material relating to said Licensed Products after all required approvals have been given by the Licensor, the Licensee shall submit, at its own cost, an additional eight (8) sets of the aforementioned Production Samples or the Licensed Products and/or Promotional and Packaging Material to the Licensor.	An additional set of samples must be submitted by the Licensee after commencement of production to ensure compliance with the quality control provisions and, if necessary, to provide appropriate samples for supporting trademark applications.
(g) The Licensor may, periodically during the Term of this Agreement, require that the Licensee submit to the Licensor, at no cost to the Licensor, up to six (6) additional sets of Production Samples of the Licensed Products and/or the Promotional and Packaging Material relating to said Licensed Products for subsequent review of the quality of and copyright, patent and trademark usage and notice on same and for any	This is an ongoing requirement for the periodic submission of additional samples to ensure that the quality control requirements are being complied with.

PROVISION	COMMENTARY
other purpose that the Licensor deems appropriate.	
(h) After the required approval of Production Samples has been secured, the Licensee shall not depart therefrom in any respect without first obtaining the express prior written approval of the Licensor. The Licensee shall make submissions to the Licensor and obtain approvals in the manner required above each time new or revised concept, layouts, descriptions, artwork, models, prototype samples and/or Production Samples are created, developed and/or adopted by and/or for the Licensee.	It is important to require the Licensee not to depart in any material way from the original approved sample and this paragraph reinforces this requirement.
(i) To assure that the provisions of this Agreement are being observed, the Licensee agrees that it will allow the Licensor or its designees to enter the Licensee's premises and/or the premises where the Licensed Products are being manufactured during regular business hours and upon reasonable notice, for the purpose of inspecting the Licensed Products and the Promotional and Packaging Material relating to the Licensed Products and the facilities in which the Licensed Products and/or Promotional and Packaging Material are being manufactured and in which the Licensed Products are being packaged.	Pursuant to this paragraph, the Licensor is given a reasonable right to inspect the manufacturing facilities to ensure that the quality control requirements are being complied with.
(j) In the event that the quality standards and/or trademark, patent and copyright usage and notice requirements hereinabove referred to are not met or, in the event that said quality standards and/or trademark, patent and copyright usage and notice requirements are not maintained throughout the period of manufacture, offering for sale, sale, advertising, promotion, shipment and/or dis-	In the event that the notice or quality control requirements are not being complied with, the Licensor may require that the Licensee immediately discontinue all manufacturing and sale of the Licensed products until such requirements are met.

PROVISION	COMMENTARY
tribution of any Licensed Products hereunder, then, upon receipt of written notice from the Licensor, the Licensee shall immediately discontinue any and all manufacture, offering-for-sale, sale, advertising, promotion, shipment and distribution of the Licensed Products in connection with which the said quality standards and/or trademark, patent and copyright usage and notice requirements have not been met.	
7. *ARTWORK*	
(a) The form and content of all artwork as used by the Licensee shall be subject to the prior express written approval of the Licensor prior to its use by the Licensee. If the Licensee desires to use artwork previously approved by the Licensor on a different Licensed Product or on different Promotional and Packaging Material, the Licensee shall first submit samples of such proposed use to the Licensor for approval thereof.	The Licensee, under this paragraph, is required to obtain the Licensor's approval for the use of all artwork.
(b) All artwork and designs and/or Trademarks, or any reproductions thereof, shall, notwithstanding their invention or use by the Licensee, be and remain the property of the Licensor who shall be entitled to use and license to use such artwork and designs, subject to the provisions of this Agreement.	This reinforces the fact that the artwork is owned by the Licensor and the Licensee's use thereof is governed by this agreement.
8. *OWNERSHIP OF RIGHTS*	
(a) It is understood and agreed that the Licensor is the sole and exclusive owner of all right, title and interest in and to the Property and/or the Trademarks.	This provision recites that the Licensor is the sole owner of the Property and Trademarks.
(b) Nothing contained in this Agreement shall be construed as an assignment to the Licensee of any right, title and/or	This recites that the Agreement is a license and not an assignment and the

PROVISION	COMMENTARY
interest in and to the Property and/or to the Trademarks, it being understood that all right, title and interest relating thereto are expressly reserved by the Licensor except for the rights being licensed hereunder.	Licensor specifically reserves any rights not otherwise being licensed to the Licensee.
(c) No license as to any products other than with respect to the Licensed Products and only in the Licensed Territory is being granted hereunder and Licensor reserves for use as it may determine all rights of any kind other than the rights herein licensed to the Licensee. Licensee recognizes that Licensor may already have entered into, and may, in the future, enter into, license agreements with respect to the Property and/or the Trademarks for products which fall into the same general product category as one or more of the Licensed Products and which may be similar to but not the same as one or more of the Licensed Products in terms of use, function, or otherwise, and Licensee hereby expressly concedes that the existence of said licenses does not and shall not constitute a breach of this Agreement by the Licensor.	This is a reservation of rights clause by the Licensor for rights other than those being licensed herein. It recognizes that this Agreement is part of an overall licensing program and that similar licenses may be granted and do not constitute a breach of the agreement by the Licensor.
(d) The Licensee shall not use the Licensor's name, the Property and/or the Trademarks other than as permitted hereunder and, in particular, shall not incorporate the Licensor's name, the Property and/or the Trademarks in the Licensee's corporate or business name in any manner whatsoever. The Licensee agrees that in using the Property and Trademarks, it will in no way represent that it has any rights, title and/or interest in and/or to the Property and/or the Trademarks other than those	This provision limits the Licensee's use of the Licensor's name, Property and/or Trademark.

PROVISION	COMMENTARY
expressly granted under the terms of this Agreement. The Licensee further agrees that it will not use and/or authorize the use, either during or after the Term of this Agreement, of any configuration, trademark, trade name or other designation confusingly similar to the Licensor's Name, the Property and/or the Trademarks.	
(e) During the Term of this Agreement and thereafter, the Licensee shall not contest or otherwise challenge or attack the Licensor's rights in the Property or the Trademarks or the validity of the License being granted herein.	License estoppel is still alive and well in the trademark area and this provision requires that the Licensee may not attack the validity of the Licensor's rights in the Property and/or the Trademark.

9. GOOD WILL AND PROMOTIONAL VALUE

PROVISION	COMMENTARY
(a) The Licensee recognizes the value of the good will associated with the Property and/or the Trademarks and acknowledges that the Property and/or the Trademarks, and all rights therein and the good will pertaining thereto, belong exclusively to the Licensor. The Licensee further recognizes and acknowledges that the Property and/or the Trademarks have acquired secondary meaning in the mind of the public.	As a merchandising license agreement includes a license under the Trademarks, it is suggested that the Licensee specifically recognize the value of the good will associated with the Property and/or Trademarks and that the Trademarks have acquired secondary meaning. This is particularly helpful in the case of unregistered Trademarks.
(b) The Licensee agrees that its use of the Property and/or the Trademarks shall inure to the benefit of the Licensor and that the Licensee shall not, at any time, acquire any rights in the Property and/or the Trademarks by virtue of any use it may make of the Property and/or of the Trademarks.	A provision that Licensee's use will inure to the benefit of the Licensor is required in any form of tradmark licensing.

PROVISION	COMMENTARY
(c) The Licensee acknowledges that the Licensor is entering into this Agreement not only in consideration of the Royalties paid hereunder but also for the promotional value to be secured by the Licensor for the Property and/or the trademarks as a result of the manufacture, offering for sale, sale, advertising, promotion, shipment and distribution of the Licensed Products by the Licensee. Accordingly, the Licensee acknowledges that its failure to manufacture, offer for sale, sell, advertise, promote, ship and distribute the Licensed Products in accordance with the provisions of this Agreement or to fulfill the Licensee's obligations under the provisions thereof will result in immediate and irreparable damages to the Licensor in connection with promotion of the Property and/or the Trademarks, and that the Licensor will have no adequate remedy at law for the failure by the Licensee to abide by such provisions of this Agreement. The Licensee further agrees that in the event of any breach by the Licensee, the Licensor, in addition to all other remedies available to it hereunder, shall be entitled to injunctive relief against any such breach as well as such other relief as any court with jurisdiction may deem just and proper.	This provision forms that basis of a subsequent action for a possible preliminary injunction by the Licensor against the Licensee's subsequent, unlicensed use of the Property and/or Trademark. It includes a consent to an injunction in the event of a breach of this agreement.

10. *TRADEMARK, PATENT AND COPYRIGHT PROTECTION*

(a) The License granted hereunder is conditioned upon the Licensee's full and complete compliance with the provisions of the trademark, patent and copyright laws of the United States and the foreign country or countries in the Licensed Territory. The Licensee	This conditions the license grant upon the Licensee's full compliance with the intellectual property laws of the United States and foreign countries and requires that the Li-

PROVISION	COMMENTARY

agrees to keep records of and advise the Licensor when each of the Licensed Products is first sold in each country in the Licensed Territory.

(b) The Licensor has the right, but not the obligation, to obtain at its own cost, appropriate trademark, patent and copyright protection for the Property, the Trademarks, the Licensed products and/or the Promotional and Packaging Material.

(c) The Licensee agrees to cooperate with the Licensor in protecting and defending the Property and/or the Trademarks. In the event that any claim or problem arises with respect to the protection of the Property and/or the Trademarks in the Licensed Territory, the Licensee shall promptly advise the Licensor in writing of the nature and extent of same. The Licensor has no obligation to take any action whatsoever in the event that any claim or problem arises with respect to the protection of the Property and/or the Trademarks. The Licensor shall have the election, however, to proceed with counsel of its own choice. Alternatively, the Licensor may, at the Licensor's own expense, have the Licensee proceed on its behalf with respect to any such claim or problem, provided, however, that the Licensor's prior express written permission shall be obtained by the Licensee prior to incurring any costs chargeable to the Licensor in connection therewith.

(d) The Licensee agrees that it shall not at any time apply for any copyright, trademark or patent protection which would

---

COMMENTARY:

censee advise the Licensor upon commencement of sale of Licensed Products in any country.

The Licensor may, but is not required to, obtain appropriate patent, trademark and copyright protection for the Property and/or Trademark.

Licensee cooperation is necessary in any infringement action and is required pursuant to the terms of this paragraph.

The Licensee may never apply for patent, copyright or trademark

PROVISION	COMMENTARY
affect the Licensor's ownership of any rights in the Property and/or the Trademarks; nor file any document with any government authority or take any other action which could affect the Licensor's ownership of the Property and/or the Trademarks, or aid or abet anyone else in doing so.	protection or take any other action which would affect the Licensor's rights to the Property and/or Trademarks.

11. *INFRINGEMENTS*

(a) The Licensee agrees to assist the Licensor in the enforcement of any rights of the Licensor in the Property and/or the Trademarks. The Licensor, if it so desires, may commence or prosecute any claim or suits in its own name or in the name of the Licensee or join the Licensee as a party thereto. The Licensee agrees to notify the Licensor in writing of any infringements or imitations by third parties of the Property, the Trademarks, the Licensed Products and/or the Promotional and Packaging Material which may come to the Licensee's attention. The Licensor shall have sole right to determine whether or not any action shall be taken on account of any such infringement or imitation.

Licensee assistance is required in the event of third party infringement; however, the Licensor has the sole right to determine what action, if any, should be taken.

(b) With respect to all claims and suits, including suits in which the Licensee is joined as a party, the Licensor shall have the sole right to employ counsel of its choosing and to direct the handling of the litigation and any settlement thereof. The Licensor shall be entitled to receive and retain all amounts awarded as damages, profits or otherwise in connection with such suits.

The Licensor should take the lead in any infringement action and is entitled to retain all amounts awarded as a result thereof. In the absence of such a provision, it is questionable whether this Licensee would be entitled to a share of such proceeds.

12. *INDEMNIFICATION*

(a) The Licensor hereby agrees to defend, indemnify and hold the Licensee harmless against any claims, demands,

Indemnification by the Licensor is typically required in the event of a

PROVISION	COMMENTARY
causes of action and judgments arising solely out of the use of the Property and/or the Trademarks by the Licensee as authorized in this Agreement, provided that the Licensee shall give notice to the Licensor within ten (10) days after notification of each such claim, demand, cause of action or judgment and further provided that the Licensor shall have the right to undertake and conduct the defense of any cause of such action so brought and handle any such claim or demand.	claim by a third party challenging the Licensor's ownership of the property. In such event, the Licensor will provide a complete defense for the Licensee and pay whatever recovery may be awarded against both parties.
(b) The Licensee hereby agrees to defend, indemnify and hold the Licensor and/or any of its related entities harmless against any and all claims, demands, causes of action and judgments arising out of Licensee's design, manufacture, distribution, shipment, advertising, promotion, offering-for-sale and/or sale of the Licensed Products and/or the Promotional and Packaging Material. With respect to the foregoing indemnity, the Licensee agrees to defend and hold the Licensor harmless at no cost or expense to the Licensor whatsoever including, but not limited to, attorney's fees and court costs. The Licensor shall have the right to defend any such action or proceeding with attorneys of its own selection.	In the event of a defect in the Licensed Products, the Licensee agrees to provide a complete defense to the Licensor against claims by third parties and pay any eventual recovery.

13. *INSURANCE*

The Licensee shall, throughout the Term of this Agreement, obtain and maintain at its own cost and expense from a qualified insurance company licensed to do business in the State of New York, standard Product Liability Insurance, the form of which must be acceptable to the Licensor, naming the Licensor as an addi-	As many Licensees are unable to live up to the terms of the indemnification provision of the agreement due to their size, Licensors will typically require that the Licensee maintain product liability insurance nam-

PROVISION	COMMENTARY
tional named insured. Such policy shall provide protection against any and all claims, demands and causes of action arising out of any defects or failure to perform, alleged or otherwise, of the Licensed Products or any material used in connection therewith or any use thereof. The amount of coverage shall be in the amount recited in Schedule A attached hereto. The policy shall provide for ten (10) days notice to the Licensor from the insurer by Registered or Certified Mail, return receipt requested, in the event of any modification, cancellation or termination. The Licensee agrees to furnish the Licensor a certificate of insurance evidencing same within thirty (30) days after execution of this Agreement, and in no event shall the Licensee manufacture, offer for sale, sell, advertise, promote, ship and/or distribute the Licensed Products prior to receipt by the Licensor of such evidence of insurance.	ing the Licensor as a named insured. The amount is specified in Schedule A.

14. *EXPLOITATION BY THE LICENSEE*

PROVISION	COMMENTARY
(a) The Licensee agrees to commence distribution, shipment and sale of all of the Licensed Products in commercially reasonable quantities in each of the countries in the Licensed Territory on or before the Initial Shipment date recited in Schedule A attached hereto.	As provided in Schedule A, the Licensee must commence the sale of Licensed Products on or before the Initial Shipment Date.
(b) The Licensee further agrees that during all Terms of this Agreement, the Licensee will continue to diligently and continuously distribute, ship and sell all of the Licensed Products in all countries in the Licensed Territory and that it will use its best efforts to make and maintain adequate arrangements for the distribution, shipment and sale necessary to meet the demand for all such Licensed Products in all countries of the Licensed Territory.	This provision requires that after introducing Licensed Products, the Licensee continues to diligently ship and sell Licensed Products in all countries in the Licensed Territory. Under subsequent termination provisions, failure to continuously ship and sell will result in termination of at least a portion of the Agreement.

PROVISION	COMMENTARY
(c) The Licensee agrees that the Licensed Products will be sold, shipped and distributed outright, at a competitive price that does not exceed the price generally and customarily charged the trade by the Licensee, and not on an approval, consignment, sale or return basis. The Licensee will not discriminate against the Licensed Products by granting commissions/discounts to salesmen, dealers and/or distributors in favor of Licensee's other products. The Licensee further agrees that the Licensed Products will only be sold to jobbers, wholesalers and distributors for sale, shipment and distribution to retail stores and merchants and/or to retail stores and merchants for sale, shipment and distribution direct to the public.	This provision protects the Licensor against the Licensee's sale of Licensed Products at below market cost.

15. *PREMIUMS,   PROMOTIONS   AND SECONDS*

(a) The Licensor shall have and retain the sole and exclusive right to utilize, or license third parties to utilize, any of the Licensed Products in connection with any premium, giveaway, mail order, in-theatre sales, promotional arrangement or fan club (collectively referred to as "Promotional Products"), which retained right may be exercised by the Licensor concurrently with the rights licensed to the Licensee hereunder.	Premium and promotional sales are specifically excluded from the license Agreement.
(b) The Licensee agrees not to offer for sale, sell, ship, advertise, promote, distribute and/or use for any purpose whatsoever and/or to permit any third party to offer for sale, sell, ship, advertise, promote, distribute and/or use for any purpose whatsoever any Licensed Products and/or Promotional and Packaging Material relating to the Licensed	The Licensee is not permitted to sell any Licensed Products which fail to meet the quality control requirements of this Agreement or which are otherwise defective or damaged.

PROVISION	COMMENTARY

Products which are damaged, defective, seconds, or otherwise fail to meet the specifications and/or quality standards and/or trademark, patent and copyright usage and notice requirements of this Agreement.

16. *ASSIGNABILITY AND SUB-LICENSING*

(a) The License granted hereunder is and shall be personal to the Licensee and shall not be assigned by any act of the Licensee or by operation of law. The Licensee shall not have the Licensed Products manufactured for the Licensee by a third party unless the Licensee first obtains the Licensor's prior express written approval. The Licensee shall have no right to grant any sub-licenses without the Licensor's prior express written approval. Any attempt on the part of Licensee to arrange for manufacture by a third party or to sublicense or assign to third parties its rights under this Agreement shall constitute a material breach of this Agreement.

> As recited above, the Agreement is personal to the Licensee and cannot be assigned without the Licensor's prior express written approval. Similarly, the Licensee cannot sublicense third parties without Licensor approval.

(b) The Licensor shall have the right to assign its rights and obligations under this Agreement without the approval of the Licensee.

> The Licensor should retain the right to assign its right without Licensee approval.

17. *TERMINATION*

The following termination rights are in addition to the termination rights provided elsewhere in this Agreement:

(a) *Immediate Right of Termination.* The Licensor shall have the right to immediately terminate this Agreement by giving written notice to the Licensee if the Licensee does any of the following:

> This governs the grounds under which the Agreement may be immediately terminated upon written notice to the Licensee.

(i) Manufactures, offers for sale, sells, advertises, promotes, ships, distributes and/or uses in any way any Licensed

> If the Licensee manufactures or sells any product or uses any Promotional

PROVISION	COMMENTARY
Product and/or Promotional and Packaging Material without having the prior written approval of the Licensor as provided for by the provisions of this Agreement, or continues to manufacture, offer for sale, sell, advertise, promote, ship, distribute and/or use in any way any Licensed Product and/or Promotional and Packaging Material after receipt of notice from the Licensor disapproving and/or withdrawing approval of same;	Material without prior approval of the Licensor, the Licensor can immediately terminate this Agreement.
(ii) Becomes subject to any voluntary or involuntary order of any governmental agency involving the recall of any of the Licensed Products and/or Promotional and Packaging Material because of safety, health or other hazards or risks to the public;	In the event of a government recall of any Licensed Product, the Licensor can immediately terminate this Agreement.
(iii) It or its controlling shareholders or any of its officers, directors or employees take any actions in connection with the manufacture, offering for sale, sale, advertising, promotion, shipment and/or distribution of the Licensed Products and/or the Promotional and Packaging Material which damages or reflects adversely upon the Licensor, the Property and/or the Trademarks;	In the event of any adverse action against the Licensor, the Property and/or the Trademark by the Licensee, the Licensor has the right to immediately terminate this Agreement.
(iv) Breaches any of the provisions of this Agreement relating to the unauthorized assertion of rights in the Property and/or the Trademarks;	Should the Licensee make any unauthorized assertion of rights in the Property and/or Trademark, the Licensor may immediately terminate this Agreement.
(v) Two or more times during a twelve-month period fails to make timely payment of Royalties when due or fails to make timely submission of Royalty statements when due;	The Licensor may terminate the Agreement if the Licensee repeatedly fails to make timely payments of royalty when due.

PROVISION	COMMENTARY
(vi) Breaches any of the provisions of this Agreement prohibiting the Licensee from directly or indirectly arranging for manufacture by third parties, assigning, transferring, sublicensing or otherwise encumbering this Agreement or any of its rights or obligations thereunder; and	Should the Licensee assign or sublicense its rights, this constitutes grounds for termination.
(vii) Fails to obtain or maintain product liability insurance as required by the provisions of this Agreement.	In the event of the Licensee's failure to maintain product liability insurance, the Licensor may immediately terminate this Agreement.
(b) *Immediate Right to Terminate a Portion of This Agreement.* The Licensor shall have the right to immediately terminate the portion(s) of this Agreement relating to any Licensed Product(s) and any countries of the Licensed Territory in connection with which the Licensee, for any reason, fails to commence sale, shipment and distribution of any such Licensed Product(s) in any such portion in accordance with the terms of this Agreement.	The Licensor may terminate a portion of the Agreement with regard to a specific Licensed Product and/or a specific Licensed Territory in the event of the Licensee's failure to commence or maintain sales of that Product or within that country.
(c) *Right to Terminate on Notice.* This Agreement may be terminated by either party upon thirty (30) days written notice to the other party in the following events, provided that during the thirty (30) day period, the defaulting party fails to cure the breach;	The agreement may be terminated by either party on 30 days written notice to the other party upon the happening of any of the subsequent events if the breach is not cured within the notice period.
(i) The Licensor shall have the right to terminate the portion(s) of this Agreement relating to any Licensed Products and any portion of the Licensed Territory if the Licensee, for any reason, after the commencement of sale, shipment and distribution of such Licensed	If the Licensee fails to continuously sell and ship Licensed Products for two consecutive Royalty Periods, the Agreement may be terminated by the Licensor on 30 days notice.

PROVISION	COMMENTARY
Products in such Licensed Territory, fails to continue to sell, ship and distribute such Licensed Products in commercially acceptable quantities in the Licensed Territory for two consecutive Royalty Periods;	
(ii) The Licensor shall have the right to terminate this Agreement if the Licensee shall violate any of its obligations under this Agreement including its payment obligations;	The Agreement may likewise be terminated in the event that the Licensee fails to make timely payment of its payment obligations.
(iii) The Licensor shall have the right to terminate this Agreement if the Licensee shall fail to pay its Minimum Royalty obligation;	In the event that the Licensee fails to pay its Minimum Royalty obligation, the Agreement is terminable on 30 days notice.
(iv) The Licensor shall have the right to terminate this Agreement if the Licensee files a petition in bankruptcy or is adjudicated a bankrupt or insolvent, or makes an assignment for the benefit of creditors, or an arrangement pursuant to any bankruptcy law, or if the Licensee discontinues its business or if a receiver is appointed for the Licensee or for the Licensee's business and such receiver is not discharged within thirty (30) days;	In the event of a bankruptcy by the Licensee, the Agreement may be terminated. There is, however, doubt whether this provision is enforceable under the Bankruptcy Act.
(v) Either party shall have the right to terminate this Agreement in the event that the other party commits a material breach of any other provision of this Agreement and said material breach is not cured within the thirty (30) day notice period.	This is a broad, all-encompassing provision providing for material breaches of the Agreement.
18. *POST-TERMINATION AND EXPIRATION RIGHTS AND OBLIGATIONS*	
(a) If this Agreement is terminated under Paragraphs 17(a) and/or (b), the Licensee and its receivers, representatives, trustees, agents, administrators,	No sell-off right is granted if the Agreement is terminated for cause. If the agreement is terminated as

PROVISION	COMMENTARY
successors and/or permitted assigns of the Licensee shall have no right to manufacture, offer for sale, sell, ship, advertise, promote and/or distribute Licensed Products or to use in any way any Promotional and Packaging Material relating to the Licensed Products.	provided above, there is no right given the Licensee to continue to manufacture and sell Licensed Products other than pursuant to this Agreement.
(b) Upon termination or expiration of this Agreement, notwithstanding anything to the contrary herein, all Royalties on sales, shipments and/or distributions theretofore made shall become immediately due and payable and no Advance or Minimum Royalty paid to Licensor shall be refunded.	Upon termination or expiration, all payment obligations are accelerated and become immediately due.
(c) After termination or expiration of this Agreement under any provision other than paragraph 17(a) and/or 17(b), the Licensee may dispose of all Licensed Products which are on hand or in the process of manufacture at the time notice of termination is received or upon the expiration of the ten in effect Term for a period of sixty (60) days after notice of termination or such expiration, as the case may be, provided that the Advances and Royalties with respect to that period are paid and the appropriate statements are furnished for that period. During such sixty (60) day period, the Licensor may itself use or license the use of the Property and/or the Trademarks in any manner at any time anywhere in the world as the Licensor sees fit.	In the event of termination or expiration other than for the enumerated grounds of paragraphs 17(a) and 17(b), a 60 day sell-off period is granted. This period is negotiable and may be extended if agreed to by the parties.
(d) After the expiration or termination of this Agreement, all rights granted to the Licensee shall forthwith revert to the Licensor, who shall be free to license others to use the Property and/or the Trademarks in connection with the	Upon expiration, the Licensor is free to contract with third parties and the Licensee may not use the Property and/or Trademark in any manner except as

PROVISION	COMMENTARY
manufacture, offering for sale, sale, advertising, promotion, shipment and/or distribution of the Licensed Products, and the Licensee shall refrain from further use of the Property and/or the Trademarks or any further reference to them, either directly or indirectly, in connection with the manufacture, offering for sale, sale, advertising, promotion, shipment and/or distribution of the Licensee's products. The Licensee shall further turn over to the Licensor all molds and other materials which reproduce the Licensed Products and/or Promotional and Packaging Material relating to the Licensed Products or shall give the Licensor satisfactory evidence of their destruction. The Licensee shall be responsible to the Licensor for any damages caused by the unauthorized use by the Licensee or by others of such molds or reproduction materials which are not turned over to the Licensor.	provided in the Agreement. The Licensee further agrees to turn over to the Licensor all material used in the manufacture of the Licensed Products or certify the destruction of same. The Licensee takes responsibility for any damage caused by the unauthorized use by the Licensee or other of such molds or reproduction materials.
(e) The Licensee acknowledges that its failure to cease the manufacture, offering for sale, sale, advertising, promotion, shipment and/or distribution of the Licensed Products and/or use in any way of the Promotional and Packaging Material relating to the Licensed Products at the termination or expiration of this Agreement will result in immediate and irreparable damage to the Licensor and to the rights of any subsequent licensee of the Licensor. The Licensee acknowledges and admits that there is no adequate remedy at law for failure to cease such activities and the Licensee agrees that in the event of such failure, the Licensor shall be enti-	This provision is a consent to injunctive relief by the Licensee in the event of a breach of the above requirement.

PROVISION	COMMENTARY
tled to equitable relief by way of injunctive relief and such other relief as any court with jurisdiction may deem just and proper.	

19. *FINAL STATEMENT UPON TERMINATION OR EXPIRATION*

Within thirty (30) days after termination or expiration of this Agreement, as the case may be, the Licensee shall deliver to the Licensor a statement indicating the number and description of the Licensed Products which it had on hand or was in the process of manufacturing as of the expiration or termination date. The Licensor shall have the option of conducting a physical inventory at the time of expiration or termination and/or at a later date in order to ascertain or verify such statement. In the event that the Licensee refuses to permit the Licensor to conduct such physical inventory, the Licensee shall forfeit its rights hereunder to dispose of such inventory. In addition to such forfeiture, the Licensor shall have recourse to all other remedies available to it.	Upon termination or expiration, the Licensee should provide the Licensor with a statement indicating the quantity of Licensed Products on hand at the time of termination. The Licensor reserves the right to conduct a physical inventory or inspection to confirm same.

20. NOTICES

All notices or other communications required or desired to be sent to either party shall be in writing and sent by Registered or Certified Mail, postage prepaid, return receipt requested, or by telex or telegram, charges prepaid to the above-recited addresses. Either party may change such address by notice in writing to the other party.	This is a classic notice provision and governs how notice and payment shall be made.

21. *RELATIONS OF THE PARTIES*

This Agreement does not create a partnership or joint venture between the parties and the Licensee shall have no power to obligate or bind the Licensor in any manner whatsoever.	The agreement is a license and not a joint venture or partnership.

PROVISION	COMMENTARY

22. APPLICABLE LAW AND DISPUTE

This Agreement shall be governed by the law of the State of New York and any claims arising hereunder shall be resolved by arbitration in New York City in accordance with the then-in-effect rules of the American Arbitration Association.

In any dispute the law of the Licensee's home state should govern. Disputes may be resolved by arbitration in New York City.

23. CAPTIONS

The captions used in connection with the paragraphs and subparagraphs of this Agreement are inserted only for purpose of reference. Such captions shall not be deemd to govern, limit, modify or in any other manner affect the scope, meaning or intent of the provisions of this Agreement or any part thereof nor shall such captions otherwise be given any legal affect.

This is a broad provision specifying that the captions for each paragraph are for reference purposes only and have no legal affect.

24. WAIVER

(a) No waiver by either party of a breach or a default hereunder shall be deemed a waiver by such party of a subsequent breach or default of a like or similar nature.

A waiver of a breach will not constitute a subsequent waiver by that party of like or similar breaches.

(b) Resort by the Licensor to any remedies referred to in this Agreement or arising by reason of a breach of this Agreement by the Licensee shall not be construed as a waiver by the Licensor of its right to resort to any and all other legal and equitable remedies available to the Licensor.

Similarly, the failure to pursue one particular remedy should not constitute a waiver of other remedies available to the Licensor.

25. SURVIVAL OF THE RIGHTS

Notwithstanding anything to the contrary contained herein, such obligations which remain executory after expiration of the Term of this Agreement shall remain in full force and effect until discharged by performance and such rights as pertain thereto shall remain in force until their expiration.

Certain provisions of the agreement extend after its natural expiration and, as such, the agreement should remain executory until fully discharged.

PROVISION	COMMENTARY

26. *SEVERABILITY*

In the event that any term or provision of this Agreement shall for any reason be held to be invalid, illegal or unenforceable in any respect, such invalidity, illegality or unenforceability shall not affect any other term or provision and this Agreement shall be interpreted and construed as if such term or provision, to the extent the same shall have been held to be invalid, illegal or unenforceable, had never been contained herein.

This provides that in the event that a provision in the agreement is held invalid or unenforceable, it will be deemed severed from the Agreement and the remaining provisions of the agreement will remain in effect.

27. *INTEGRATION*

This Agreement represents the entire understanding between the parties hereto with respect to the subject matter hereof and this Agreement supersedes all previous representations, understandings or agreements, oral or written, between the parties with respect to the subject matter hereof and cannot be modified except by a written instrument signed by the parties hereto.

By their execution below, the parties hereto have agreed to all of the terms and conditions of this Agreement.

Integration means that the agreement is a final document and the parties cannot rely on earlier drafts or understandings. Similarly, the agreement may not be modified or changed except in writing signed by both parties.

PENNFAIR PRODUCTIONS, INC.

By: _____

Title: _____

Date: _____

BESTBILT PRODUCTS, INC.

By: _____

Title: _____

Date: _____

APPENDIX B

LICENSING POTENTIAL IN A CONSUMER PRODUCTS COMPANY

"American Oats Company"

Licensing Evaluation Report

With changes made where appropriate, what follows is an actual brand extension/licensing evaluation report produced for a consumer products company (American Oats is a fictional substitute) by Conposit, a team of licensing consultants with which I (Tom Meyer) am involved.* The company and brand name changes, and other changes, are the authors'.

I. Background Objectives

The overall objective of this program is to provide an *ongoing* and disciplined licensing activity for the American Oats Company (A.O.C.) which would expand the utility and profitability of existing brands while strengthening their position and usage in the marketplace. Specifically, the desire is to provide:

1. Increased marketing efficiencies.
2. New channels of distribution.
3. New products and line extensions utilizing technology or manufacturing outside normal A.O.C. manufacturing capabilities.
4. Diversification outside the confines of existing basic businesses.
5. New revenue centers with significant royalties.
6. Means to expand and solidify brand imagery for existing basic businesses.

---

* Reprinted with the full permission of Conposit, Six The Pines Court, Creve Coeur, Missouri 63141.

7. Support of sales force efforts with the trade.
8. Strengthening of employee identification with American Oats Company.

Stage I of the program is designed to develop hypothetical areas of opportunity based on A.O.C. brand equities and offer a reasonable evaluation of the overall potential of a brand extension (licensing) program.

The remainder of this report will deal with:

II. Overall Evaluation of the Program.
III. Hypothetical Areas of Opportunity—Development Process.
IV. Hypothetical Areas of Opportunity and Associated Initial "Concepts."
V. Issues to be Addressed in Primary Research in the Second Stage of the Program.

It should be kept in mind that the entire purpose of the Stage I review is to provide a foundation for Stage II research. The assumptions made and hypotheses drawn may and probably *will* change dramatically after research is complete. We wish to establish the topics of discussion for research and provide *stimulus* which might facilitate discussion during Stage I review.

The overall evaluation of the program is at this time largely subjective. The positive evaluation is, however, justified when equities of A.O.C. and its brands are viewed in conjunction with the large array of sources of dollar volume against which they might be applied.

II. *Overall Evaluation of the Project Potential*

The potential of the licensing project for A.O.C. is considerable. There is little, if any, question that its eventual output will more than justify the time and resources expended on its behalf. This judgment is based upon a review of A.O.C. equities and a knowledge of several categories in food as well as those outside of food which can be exploited by utilizing those equities. Below are general statements which can be made about the very real possibilities of A.O.C. licensing efforts in the future. Justification for future pursuit of the program includes, but is not limited to the following:

- Increase visual recognition of key products: American Oat Loaf/Molly O's graphics; reinforce existing advertising and impact at the point of sale.
- Open new channels of distribution for oat products and related items.
- Dollar volume of food categories that can be addressed is aggregate one billion plus *incremental*.
- Collateral opportunities exist that might generate substantial royalties (which may be viewed as almost straight bottom-line profit) in the area of

one million in years one and two, and three to four million per annum as the program proceeds.
- More important is the fact that these collateral opportunities directly reinforce or expand A.O.C. brand imagery.
- There is a chance to exploit and enhance the leadership image of American Oat Loaf/Molly O's and utilize this both *internally* for incentive and against consumers as promotional goods, etc.

The judgments above are supported by the output of the interim concept generation conducted.

III. Hypothetical Areas of Opportunity—Development Process
The eventual areas of opportunity which will serve as focus for generation and as a means of soliciting and screening submissions will be developed with the aid of qualitative research.

In order to make that research optimally efficient and productive, we *first* created "hypothetical areas of opportunity" and identified specific issues to be addressed. This will, of course, help us in conducting useful targeted discussions and provide stimulus material to promote consumer response during these discussions.

The process by which the hypothetical areas of opportunity were developed was relatively simple. It involved a review and combinations of five basic areas of information:

A. A.O.C. tangible equities.
B. A.O.C. brand image equities.
C. A.O.C. needs/objectives.
D. Sources of dollar volume.
E. Consumer purchase and usage dynamics.

The pages which follow will outline the *principal* information developed and utilized during the development of hypothetical areas of opportunity.

A. A.O.C. Tangible Equities
   1. Equities
      The *tangible* corporate equities of A.O.C. considered to be most important in this initial development stage were:
- Unequaled direct store delivery system.
- Considerable leverage in convenience-store distribution.
- R&D/manufacturing capabilities in volume output, packaging, formulation, baking, etc.
- Marketing, advertising, promotion expertise.
- High unit volume and associated package movement.

2. *Implications*

The implications of these equities to a program of licensing are somewhat obvious and include, but are not limited to, the following:

- The direct store delivery system could easily add value to items other than current franchise items which demand "freshness," or which have relatively short shelf lives.
- This same delivery system could be used as a tangible part of negotiations with possible joint venture partners who have product capabilities but no effective means of achieving grocery short-shelf-life distribution.
- Convenience-store leverage could also add to the impact of A.O.C. brand equities to potential licensees with capabilities in bakery-related, or other than bakery, goods.
- The versatility in formulating and baking products suggest that A.O.C. could extend entries in its bakery and oatmeal products *beyond* current *types* (breads, cookies, sweet snacks, breakfast oatmeal) or price levels. The capabilities suggest that there are several food entries that could be produced which do not currently "fit" under American Oat Loaf/Molly O's branding. This, in turn, suggests two very important needs:
  - Extend the product image equities of American Oat Loaf/Molly O's brands to accommodate "high end," "gourmet," "health," or "speciality" goods.
  - Obtain a new brand name.
  - The expertise in marketing, advertising, promotion and related support activities could also be used as a tangible part of any negotiation with licensees or joint venture partner.
  - The expertise mentioned above in combination with package movement suggests a *major* advantage in promoting any collateral goods manufactured under license.

B. *A.O.C. Brand Image Equities*

This consideration is, of course, at the very heart of any licensing effort. The equities (and, in some cases, the liabilities) of individual brands will in large part determine how they should be employed in a disciplined program of learning. For it is only by an appreciation of what intangible effects a brand might have or lack that we can identify categories, and individual items and suppliers within those categories, which can best *utilize the A.O.C. brands* or, in turn, *offer image enhancement to those brands*.

1. *Equities and Liabilities*

The major equities and liabilities of each brand in this consideration case are *hypothesized* to be:

Positive	Neutral	Negative

a. American Oat Loaf (original)

Positive	Neutral	Negative
Everyday high quality/consistent quality	Cannot duplicate at home	Too "substantial" for little children
Most versatile brand	Fortified	If healthy, not tasty perception
Acceptable to most of family as sandwich bread		Not homemade
"Fresh"		
Softest whole-grain bread		
Leading brand—category leader		
Perceived as healthiest grain; high fiber; heart food		
Good toasting bread		

b. Molly O's (cookies; cream-filled cakes)

Positive	Neutral	Negative
Fresh	Strong association with "junk food"	Too sweet
Wholesome/ trustworthy		If healthy, not tasty perception
Allowable indulgence for kids		Perceived as "growing-kid food"
"Healthy" treat		

c. American Oat Mini-Loaves (tea; bacon; fruit and walnut; original)

Positive	Neutral	Negative
Versatile use		High-priced
Upscale		
Health breads		

d. American Country Oat Rolls

Positive	Neutral	Negative
American classic "whole-grain roll"	Hearty appetite association	Perceived as dinner roll; not sandwich roll
Stays fresh/soft		
Consistent quality		

Positive	Neutral	Negative

e. Other American Oat Company brands (beyond what they share in American Oat Loaf/Molly O's parentage)

i. American Oat Meals

Positive	Neutral	Negative
Variety breakfast		Packaging makes it appear overly processed
"Healthy" Entire family appeal Easy/fast preparation		

ii. American Oat Crunchies

Positive	Neutral	Negative
High-energy snacks with fiber	Stay-fresh packaging	Cereal association
		For adults or babies?

C. A.O.C. Needs and Objectives

The needs and objectives in the case of this program will go beyond those stated in any brand's marketing plans. They are needs and objectives that are implied by brand equities and an appreciation of available sources of dollar volume. Again, it should be mentioned that these needs and objectives have been hypothesized as ones which would be of considerable import if an ongoing program of licensing can be established.

1. General Needs
- Develop business in new distribution.
- Extend utility/profitability of direct store delivery system.
- Enhance/expand the utility of A.O.C. brand names.
- Develop significant revenue from royalties.
- Extend basic business in baked goods beyond its present target, occasion utility, and price perception.

2. Franchise/Brand Specific Needs
- Extend business into areas of "child-oriented" products/"all-family" products other than baked goods, utilizing the positive equities of American Oat Loaf or Molly O's.
- Increase adult-acceptable imagery for sweet snacks/brands.
- Increase child-acceptable imagery for health snacks/brands.
- Participate more in "specialty breads" and rolls.
- Compete more effectively with "high-end" direct store delivered goods.

- Compete more directly with "in-store bakery" for dollar volume.
- Legitimately establish increased rack space.
- Establish "Any Meal" legitimacy in image and distribution.
- Improve price–value perceptions versus lower-priced competitive snacks/competitive "everyday breads"; (primarily product imagery).
- Improve legitimate competitive stance versus *higher*-priced sweet baked goods and cookies at in-store bakery level.
- Stimulate awareness and image of American "Light" Loaves through increased retail support—image separation from American Oat Loaf—while leveraging American Oat Loaf name.
- Increase legitimate participation in the variety bread segment.
- Differentiate items in American Oat Loaf family, including American Oat Loaf Light, Mini-Loaves, etc.
- Stimulate awareness and image of American Oat Meals.

D. *Sources of Dollar Volume*

The initial categories of interest were developed with several criteria in mind. The most important of these were:
- Compatibility with A.O.C. brand product or user imagery.
- Sufficient size to warrant time/effort.
- Trade or consumer dynamics to suggest vitality or vulnerability.
- Compatibility with A.O.C. needs and objectives.
- Compatibility with tangible equities or capabilities of A.O.C.

1. *Collateral Sources*

Collateral sources of dollar volume were selected primarily by broad classification. In this case, the specific execution of a licensing concept will have a very marked effect. It is not enough, for instance, to simply offer up our brand name equities for use by a clothing manufacturer. Some central design differentation or benefit must be tied to A.O.C. equities to make the licensed entry *proprietary* and useful to the franchise:

Category	Total Sales under License ($ billions)	Licensed Sales as a % of Total Sales
Apparel and accessories	$22.6 billion	18%
Gifts and novelties	3.2	38
Home furnishings and housewares	4.5	10
Publishing and stationery	4.5	12
Sporting goods	7.8	28
Toys	8.1	64

2. Food/Grocery Products

In this early stage, screening of categories was based on *size* and some reasonable applicability to American Oat Loaf/Molly O's brands or A.O.C. tangible equities. For the most part, the categories selected seemed to have applicability to American Oat Loaf/Molly O's/Everyday Quality/For All the Family consumption patterns. Others would seem to benefit from direct store delivery or isolated equities of other A.O.C. brands such as American Oat Mini-Loaves or American Country Oat Rolls. Initial exploration will include, but not be limited to, the following:

Item	Grocery Expenditures* ($ millions)
Variety bread	$ 770 million
Crackers/cookies/biscuits	4,100
Sweet goods, baked	760
In-store bakery	4,110
Refrigerated juices	1,800
Refrigerated donuts	561
Frozen baked goods	1,070
Frozen breakfast entries	340
Ice cream novelties	1,620
Frozen dinners	1,560
Frozen vegetables	1,590
Packaged cold cuts	3,400
Frankfurters	1,600
Cake mixes and frostings	790
Cold cereals	4,200
Cereal bars	460
Toaster pastries	100
Canned/bottled juices	3,300
Jams/jellies	1,000
Peanut butter	860
Cocoa	280
Powdered drink mixes	780
Breakfast drinks	135
Fruit rolls and bars	200
Dinner mixes	620
Canned/jarred pasta	510
BBQ sauces	300
Mayo/sandwich spreads	1,100
Vitamins	1,400

* 1986 Supermarket Business Survey—retail dollars in grocery.

E. Consumer Purchase and Usage Dynamics

In addition to specific category dynamics, some general topics of purchase and usage behavior will be reviewed during generation and evaluation of concepts. These would include but not be limited to:

- "Rote" purchase behavior.
- Purchase behavior when items are primarily for consumption by children.
- "Snack" as a meal occasion and snacking in general.
- Dynamics of the breakfast meal occasion.
- Dimensions of "quality" and how it changes by category, by usage occasion, by end user.
- "Convenience" and how it varies by category, usage occasion, and end user.

IV. Hypothetical Areas of Opportunity and Initial Concepts

The areas of opportunity listed below are based upon an initial review of program objectives and criteria as well as A.O.C. brand equities. They deal with utilization of those aforementioned equities in other food categories as well as collateral/promotional goods and services.

Each area of opportunity is written in the form of a "problem" to be compatible with our generation techniques.

A. The two all-inclusive "problems" which will be kept in mind at all times throughout the program are:
  1. How to exploit the equities of A.O.C. brands in categories other than baked goods via licensing to provide business diversification, new distribution, and significant revenue from royalties or joint venture.
  2. How to utilize licensing to provide brand name exposure, image enhancement or reinforcement, advertising synergies, promotional opportunities, and significant revenue from royalties.

B. The remaining "problems" are more specific in nature and are accompanied by example(s) of specific initial "concepts" which may be used as stimulus material in Stage II research. The pages which follow list these hypothetical areas of opportunity and specific conceptual executions of each.
  1. How to best exploit American Oat Loaf/Molly O's "kids" association (middle of the road, healthy, wholesome) in collateral categories of interest:
     - Line of "Molly O" clothes for little girls (5–10); "An American Girl" image.
     - "Molly O" dolls.
     - "Oat Crunchies" line of "fun wear"—beach jams; sweatshirts; specialty hats.
     - "American Oats" line of rugged outdoor wear for boys and girls (5–10); overalls; shorts; flannel shirts.
     - "American Loafer" sleepwear.
     - Create "Molly O" Nerf toys; establish new games.

- "American Oats"/"Molly O's" lunchboxes; thermos.
- "Molly O" duffles; book bags; sleeping bags.
- "American Oatcakes" soaps.
- "American Oat Kids" wallpaper and sheets.
- "American Oat Kids" Christmas tree ornaments.
- "American Oat Kids" stationery.
- "Molly O's" life preservers.

2. How to best exploit American Oat Loaf/Molly O's association with wholesome/kids/middle-of-the-road food.
   - "American Oat Kids" vitamins.
   - "Molly O's Peanut Butter"; "Molly O's Jam."
   - "Molly O's Bread"—thinner slice; less dense.

3. How to best exploit the breakfast-meal occasion with A.O.C. associations.
   - "American Oat Crunchies Cereal."
   - "Molly O's Toaster Pastries."

4. How to best exploit snacking behavior with A.O.C. brands associations.
   - Frozen "Molly O's", ice-cream filled cookies, under license or joint venture.
   - License "Molly O" to Baskin Robbins or Dairy Queen for frozen desserts.

5. How to best utilize A.O.C. graphics in collateral materials.
   - Oatcake kites.
   - Logoed shirts.
   - Food shot jigsaw puzzles; logo jigsaw (Hallmark).

6. How to take advantage of adult familiarity with and "affection" for Molly O's/American Oat Loaf/American Oat Crunchies in collateral categories.
   - "American Oat Kids" beach towels.
   - "American Oat Company" greeting cards.
   - "American Oat Company" "surprise inside" money card "to sow a few wild oats on me."
   - Kitchen accessories: tins, napkins, placemats with American Oats graphics.
   - Molly O "snack cards" (just a note. . . .).
   - "American country" air freshener.

7. How best to employ the Molly O "sense of fun" or "allowable indulgence" in food categories.
   - "Molly O' Fruit Snacks."
   - Molly O' frozen cream pies.
   - "Molly O' Miniatures"—candy snacks.

8. How to expand American Oat Loaf/Molly O's meal-occasion equities into consumables other than baked goods.
   • "American Oat Cakes" (pancakes).
   • American Oat Co. frozen desserts.
   • American Oat Co. casserole suppers.
   • "Country Cold Cuts" for "Country Oat Rolls."

9. How to expand the possibilities of adult usage of A.O.C. products in all meal occasions.
   • A.O.C. microwave loaves.
   • American Oats breakfast rolls.

10. How to extend "Wholesome" and "American" equities of A.O.C. to other food categories.
    • American Oats bread spreads.
    • "Molly O's Veggie Dips 'N Chips."

11. How to extend the middle-of-the-road "Country" of "American Country Oat Rolls" in categories other than baked goods.
    • "American Country" frozen dinner sandwich.
    • "American Country" Shirts 'N Shorts.
    • "American Country" condiments and sauces.

12. How to best exploit the most recent nutrition information on the value of oats in the diet.
    • American Oats Light "loose fit" cotton shirts with logo.
    • American Oat-Bran Muffins.
    • American Oat Exercise Togs.
    • American Oat Company logo on exercise mats; sports hats; running shoes.

13. How to best utilize direct store delivery system to provide leverage for licensed "fresh" goods with All-American association.
    • Upscale baked-goods line under established brand with companion products from A.O.C.
    • "Fresh" breakfast coffees.
    • Seasonal goods such as "candy apples" with caramelized oat crunchie topping.

14. How to employ the direct store delivery system with other than bread products which might benefit from "fresh" associations and A.O.C. image equities.
    • Adult pastries—specialty baked items.

15. How to create other than bread/snack products under license for convenience-store distribution.
    • Country Oat Rolls microwave breakfast sandwiches.
    • Country Oat Rolls microwave lunch sandwiches.

16. How to utilize R&D manufacturing expertise in "higher end" goods.
    • Obtain upscale brand name and manufacture high-end goods under license.
17. How to create collateral products or food products which would most benefit from package cross-couponing in Molly O's or American Oat Loaf products.
    • Percent-off coupons for high-priced collateral goods such as "American Country" home furnishings.
    • Molly O's fortified juices—Molly O's dairy products.
18. How to address categories that would benefit most by association with American Oat Loaf/Molly O's, or other A.O.C. brand imagery.
    • "Fresher."
    • All-American.
    • "Country."
    • "Heart food."
19. How to identify joint-venture candidates that would have a major interest in A.O.C. brand equities and/or tangible equities.
20. How to offer manufacturers of "convenience" products distribution and brand equity assistance in convenience stores.

V. *Questions To Be Addressed in Research*

Partially to test the validity of Stage I assumptions, but primarily to refine and solidify areas of opportunity, several broad issues will be addressed in Stage II Research. These issues will include, but not be limited to, the following:

1. What quality connotations do A.O.C. brands have and how might these be extendable in food and nonfood categories?
2. What are the most leverageable equities of A.O.C. brands and to which categories are they most transferable?
3. How do Molly O's vary in image from other sweet snacks? Are there other category parallels?
4. How does American Oat Loaf vary in image from other breads? Are there other category parallels?
5. Is there a positive imagery link between children and American Oat Loaf, Molly O's, Oat Crunchies, or any other A.O.C. brand? If so, what age ranges represent the greatest opportunity?
6. What graphics or logos are easily recognized by various consumer targets and what equities do they have?
7. Does A.O.C. have any particular equities in "any meal" occasions

(breakfast, packed lunch, snack, etc.) that may be exploited in "food to food" or collateral licensing?

8. Is there any familiarity with current or past A.O.C. advertising that may be exploited or augmented by licensing?

9. What are the image equities of American Oat Loaf/Molly O's brands among adults?

10. Is there any extendable "weight control"/"light" equity based on "American Oat Loaf-Light"?

11. Is there a true "Country" equity for the "American Country Oat Rolls" brand?

12. What are the image equities of "American Oat Meals"; "American Oat Crunchies"?

APPENDIX C

TRADE SHOWS AND MEETINGS FOR LICENSORS AND LICENSEES

The following trade shows and meetings, generally geared toward those involved in promotional licensing, are worth attending.* The phone numbers refer you to the sponsoring organization. Some shows are held in different regions of the country more than once a year; we list them according to the time of year they were held in 1988–89:

January

Transworld Housewares Shows (312-446-8434)
NAMSB Men's Sportswear Show (212-986-1811)
Imprinted Sportswear Show (214-239-3060)
NATPE (213-282-8801)
New York International Gift Fair (212-686-6070)

February

Super Show '89 (1-800-327-3736)
Back-to-School Merchandise Show (516-627-4000)
National Shoe Fair of America (212-246-3410)
New York International Toy Fair (212-675-1141)
National Variety Merchandise Show (212-697-3521)

March

Imprinted Sportswear Show (214-239-3060)

---

* Courtesy of *The Licensing Book* magazine, Adventure Publishing, 264 W. 40th St., New York, N.Y. 10018, $36 per year.

April

Transworld Housewares Show (312-446-8434)
Worldwide Licensing Exposition (212-575-4510)

May

Premium Incentive Show (516-627-4000)
National Stationery Show (212-686-6070)

June

American Booksellers Association Book Fair (212-463-8450)
Footwear Fashion Week (212-246-3410)
Mid-Year Variety Merchandise Show (212-676-6070)
Licensing '89 (212-484-8880)

August

National Shoe Fair (212-246-3410)
International Kids Fashion Show (212-594-0880)
VSDA Annual Convention (609-596-8500)
New York International Gift Fair (212-686-6070)
Stationery Show (415-474-2300)

September

Action Sports Retailer Trade Expo (714-499-5374)
MAGIC (213-626-0735)
NSGA Fall Trade Show (312-439-4000)
National Merchandise Show (516-627-4000)
Imprinted Sportswear Show (214-239-3060)
Action Sports Retailer Trade Expo (714-499-5374)

October

Sporting Goods Mfg. Association (305-842-4100)
Frankfurt Book Fair (212-974-8856)
MIPCOM (212-967-7600)
NSGA World Sports Expo (312-439-4000)
NAMSB Sportswear Show (212-986-1811)

November

National Bed, Bath and Linen November Market Week (212-689-5550) JPMA (609-234-9155)

December

Footwear Fashion Week and National Footwear Exposition (212-246-3410)

APPENDIX D

PROSPECTIVE LICENSEE
INFORMATION FORM

MAJOR LEAGUE BASEBALL PROPERTIES

PROSPECTIVE LICENSEE INFORMATION FORM

MAJOR LEAGUE BASEBALL®

350 Park Avenue
New York, NY 10022
(212) 371-7800

✶✶ NOTE ✶✶
This is an application, not a license.
It will be reviewed and accepted or rejected
at the sole discretion of Major League Baseball Properties.

PROSPECTIVE LICENSEE INFORMATION FORM

CIRCLE ONE – NATIONAL/LOCAL/SUPPLIER LICENSE. WHICH CLUB(S)? _____

I. **COMPANY INFORMATION**

    A. Legal Name _____

    B. Address _____

          _____

             (City)   (State)   (Zip Code)

    C. Telephone (_____) _____

    D. TWX _____ Years In Business _____

    E. Principal Contact _____ Title _____

    F. Previous Names For This Business And Businesses Operated By Any
        Principal Of This Company Within The Last 5 Years

        _____

        _____

II. **DESCRIPTION OF COMPANY**

    A. Legal Form Of Organization: Corporation   ( )
        (Check One)   S Corporation   ( )
                              Partnership   ( )
                              Limited Partnership ( )
                              Sole Proprietorship ( )
                              Trust   ( )
                              Other (please specify) ( )

                              _____

        If A Corporation, State Or Province Of Incorporation: _____
        Employer I.D. Number _____

        If A Partnership, Organized And Existing Under The Laws Of
        The State Or Province Of _____
        Name, Date Of Birth, Social Security Number Of President _____

        _____

        If Sole Proprietor, Date Of Birth, Social Security Number _____

        _____

    B. Identify All Principal Operating Officers Of Your Organization

        President   _____
        Vice President(s)   _____
                               _____
                               _____
                               _____
        Sales Director   _____
        Marketing/Advertising Director _____
        Chief Financial Officer   _____

        List All Other Owners And/Or Partners On A Separate Sheet

III. FINANCIAL INFORMATION

    A. BANK REFERENCES

        1. Name _____

           Branch _____ Account # _____

           Address _____

           Bank Contact _____

           Telephone (___)_____

        2. Name _____

           Branch _____ Account # _____

           Address _____

           Bank Contact _____

           Telephone (___)_____

    B. Credit References (Suppliers Or Vendors Who Deal With Your Firm)

        1. Name _____

           Address _____

           Telephone (___)_____

        2. Name _____

           Address _____

           Telephone (___)_____

IV. PRODUCT INFORMATION

    A. Description Of Products For Which You Seek License. Use Additional Sheet(s) If Necessary.

        Product 1 _____

        Product 2 _____

        Product 3 _____

        Product 4 _____

    B. Please Submit A Sample/Prototype Of Each Product.

    C. Estimated Wholesale Selling Price (Per Unit)

        Product 1 _____

        Product 2 _____

        Product 3 _____

        Product 4 _____

    D. Does Your Company Currently Sell The Item(s) In Question? _____

    E. Trade/Brand Names Of Products Manufactured/Sold By Your Company:

        _____

V. MANUFACTURING INFORMATION

(Note: If More Than Four Products, Use Separate Sheet(s) To Answer
All Questions For Each Product. **Hereafter We** Refer To
To Product 1 As P 1, Product 2 As P 2, etc.).

A. Where Will The Product(s) Be Manufactured?   P1   P2   P3   P4
    D = Domestic   F = Foreign   B = Both   __   __   __   __

B. Will You Manufacture?   __   __   __   __

C. If You Will <u>Not</u> Be The Manufacturer, Who Will Be?

    P 1   Name   _____
          Address   _____
                     _____
          Telephone _____
          Contact   _____ Title _____

    P 2   Name   _____
          Address   _____
                     _____
          Telephone _____
          Contact   _____ Title _____

    P 3   Name   _____
          Address   _____
                     _____
          Telephone _____
          Contact   _____ Title _____

    P 4   Name   _____
          Address   _____
                     _____
          Telephone _____
          Contact   _____ Title _____

D. If You Will Be The Manufacturer, Please Provide The Name(s) and
    Address(es) Of Your Plant(s).

    P 1   _____
          _____
          _____

    P 2   _____
          _____
          _____

    P 3   _____
          _____
          _____

    P 4   _____
          _____
          _____

VI. SALES AND DISTRIBUTION INFORMATION

A. Company's Sales For Most Recent Year (All Products) _____
   Sales Volume For Previous Year _____

B. Distribution Capability: National ( ) Regional ( ) # States ___

C. Sales Force Description. Indicate Yes Or No And Number Of People.

   1. Own Sales Force   (   )   # Of Salespersons _____
   2. Reps/Jobbers   (   )   # Of Reps/Jobbers _____
   3. Distributors   (   )   # Of Distributors _____
   4. Total Number Of Field Sales Force _____
   5. Mail Order/Direct Response   Explain _____

D. Current Distribution: National ( ) Regional ( ) # States ___

Type Of Account	Name Leading Accounts	% Of Sales Volume
1. National Chains		
2. Regional Chains		
3. Department Stores		
4. Sports Specialty		
5. Discount Stores		
6. Sporting Goods		
7. Drug Stores		
8. Food Stores		
9. Convenience Stores		
10. Team Concessionaires		
11. Toy Stores		
12. Catalogs/Direct Mail		
13. Catalog Stores		
14. Other (Specify)		

E. Estimate Of Annual Wholesale Dollar Volume Of The Items You Wish To
   Sell Under This License (By Product, If Applicable). **This Must Be
   Completed.**

	Year 1	Year 2
P 1		
P 2		
P 3		
P 4		

F. Primary Selling Season _____

G. Accounts To Whom You Plan To Sell The Licensed Product(s)
   1. _____ 4. _____
   2. _____ 5. _____
   3. _____ 6. _____

H. If You Currently Market A Similar Type Of Item, What Was Its
   Wholesale Dollar Volume For Most Recent Year? $_____

I.   Please List Three Trade Contacts To Whom You Currently Sell Product

    1.   Company _____
        Contact (Name and Title) _____
        Telephone ( ) _____

    2.   Company _____
        Contact (Name and Title) _____
        Telephone ( ) _____

    3.   Company _____
        Contact (Name and Title) _____
        Telephone ( ) _____

VII.   MARKETING INFORMATION

A.   Indicate The Marketing Promotion You Will Use To Support Your Product. Check Those Used, And, If Regional Or Local, Indicate Area.

	TV/Radio	Print	National	Local Or Regional (Indicate Area)
1. Consumer Advertising				
2. Trade Advertising				
3. In-Store Materials				
4. Sales/Trade Incentives				
5. Co-Op Advertising				
6. Other:				
Specify _____				

B.   Please Identify Your Advertising Agency.

Name _____

Address _____

Key Contact _____ Telephone ( ) _____

C.   Should You Receive The License, What Amount Do You Plan To Spend In Advertising, Promotion and Merchandising Funds In Support Of The Licensed Product(s) For the First Year? $ _____

D.   Who Is Responsible For Your Product Design And Artwork?
    _____ Telephone ( )

E.   Describe Your Quality Control Program _____
    _____
    _____

F.   Initial Marketing Date _____

G.   Date Product Is To Be Presented To Buyers _____

VIII. OTHER LICENSE INFORMATION

A. Does Your Company Market Products Under Other Licensing Contracts?
Yes _____ No _____

B. If Yes, Specify Other Licenses Below:

1. Property _____ Years Under License _____
Licensing Company _____
Address _____
_____
Key Contact _____ Telephone (____) _____

2. Property _____ Years Under License _____
Licensing Company _____
Address _____
_____
Key Contact _____ Telephone (____) _____

3. Property _____ Years Under License _____
Licensing Company _____
Address _____
_____
Key Contact _____ Telephone (____) _____

4. Property _____ Years Under License _____
Licensing Company _____
Address _____
_____
Key Contact _____ Telephone (____) _____

IX. OTHER INFORMATION

A. Have There Been Any Voluntary Or Involuntary Bankruptcies Of The
Companies Listed In Section I (A) and (F)? _____ If So,
Attach A Separate Sheet Providing All Details Including Disposition.

B. Have Any Claims Been Filed Against The Companies Listed In
Section I (A) And (F) For Trademark, Copyright or Patent
Infringements Or For Product Liability? _____ If So,
Attach A Separate Sheet Providing All Details Including Disposition.

C. Have Any Of The Companies Listed In Section I (A) and (F)
Been Subject To Proceedings Before The Federal Trade
Commission? _____ If So, Attach A Separate Sheet Providing
All Details Including Disposition.

X. SUPPLEMENTARY ITEMS:

Please Include With This Form The Following:

A. Most Recent Annual Report
B. Sales Catalog(s)
C. Miscellaneous Information About Your Company
D. Please Complete A Business Plan For The Product(s).
Format Attached.

Please review this form to be sure that all questions have been
answered. If an item does not apply, write "NA".

XI. PROSPECTIVE LICENSEE STATEMENT

1) I hereby affirm that my answers to the above questions are true and complete, except that such questions as explicitly call for estimates, plans or projections have been answered by me in good faith and to the best of my knowledge. I understand that any license which may be granted to me by Major League Baseball Properties will be subject to immediate termination, without the return of any amounts paid or the abatement of amounts due, in the event Major League Baseball Properties finds that I have supplied false, misleading, fraudulent or incomplete information.

2) I hereby acknowledge the proprietary nature of all Major League Baseball Club names, League names and logos, and I further acknowledge that all rights, title and interest to such names and logos belong to the individual Clubs, Leagues and/or Major League Baseball. I agree that I will make no use of any Major League Baseball name or logo without the prior written consent of Major League Baseball.

3) I hereby agree that my product or concept will be reviewed and accepted or rejected at Major League Baseball Properties sole discretion.

Major League Baseball Properties has agreed that any product sample(s), mock-up(s), rendering(s), etc., which I submit in support of my application will be examined only internally within the Baseball industry during the review period and promptly returned if a license is not granted. I acknowledge that from time to time Major League Baseball Properties may license other products or concepts similar to mine without obligation to me.

Name Of Individual Supplying Information _____
Title _____

Signature _____ Date _____

MAJOR LEAGUE BASEBALL PROPERTIES
PROSPECTIVE LICENSEE INFORMATION FORM

BUSINESS PLAN OUTLINE

I. Objective:

o Concise statement of what goals you are trying to meet with
this product.

o Include information with reference to size of market, major
competitors, respective shares of market and current trends.

II. Strategy:

o How, and on what product(s) or product line, the license will
be utilized.

o To what extent the license will be utilized, including:
advertising and promotional budget, packaging, POS materials,
cooperative merchandise agreements etc.

o Define specific distribution strategies with regard to key
retailers.

III. Tailored Idea:

o Specific action(s), concept(s) or program(s) that will be
employed to achieve objectives and support strategies. These
comments should be more representative of tactics than
strategy, e.g., sales meetings to announce product line(s),
sales tools, advertising, hangtags, packaging designs, POS
materials, etc.

IV. Terms Of Proposal:

o Period of time, including a marketing date.

o Territory (territories outside the U.S. must be
identified individually and require separate license).

o Product category (e.g., adult apparel, youth apparel, novelty, etc.).

o Royalty Rate - 8 1/2%

o Guarantee expressed as a function of first and second
year sales forecast.

o Sales forecasts year 1 and year 2 in wholesale dollars.

o Advance against the guarantee with a schedule of payments
for the balance due over the proposed initial term.

o Advertising/promotional budget. Be specific with regard
to dollar amounts and how they are budgeted, e.g., TV, retail,
co-op, trade promotion, POS materials, etc.

<u>MLBP USE ONLY</u>   Date Received _____

1. Category _____   ACCOUNT MANAGER _____

2. License: National   (   )
             Local   (   )   Club _____
             Regional   (   )   Club _____
             Supplier   (   )   Club _____

3. References
             D&B   (   )   Date _____
             Bank   1   (   )   Date _____
             Bank   2   (   )   Date _____
             Trade   1   (   )   Date _____
             Trade   2   (   )   Date _____
             Trade   3   (   )   Date _____
     Other Licensors   1   (   )   Date _____
     Other Licensors   2   (   )   Date _____
     Other Licensors   3   (   )   Date _____

4. Comments _____
    _____
    _____
    _____
    _____
    _____

5. Licensed Manfacturers Agreement(s) Entered Into: _____
    With: _____
          _____
          _____
          _____
          _____

GLOSSARY

"Will you give me a glossary of key licensing terms so I can understand the contract?" That's what one corporate executive asked one of us to do for him before the client's first licensing venture. What follows is that glossary. In most cases, the phrases defined below would serve as subheadings in a licensing contract, so the definitions are really descriptions of the *objectives* of contract sections and the reason for each. It should also be noted that not all licensing contracts are organized the same way. Nonetheless, each term below will find its way into almost any merchandise licensing contract.

assignment and sublicense A clear statement prohibiting the licensee from subcontracting its functions to other companies without licensor permission.

compliance (with government standards) Clause or clauses to protect the licensor by spelling out the licensee's duties regarding complying with any and all federal, state, and local standards/regulations.

exclusivity/nonexclusivity This section delineates precisely the products the licensee agrees to license as well as the exact range of usage of the trademark that is planned. Does the licensee, for example, have *sole* right to manufacture and/or market an item?

grant of license Exact wording spelling out the permission granted by the trademark owner; includes items such as trademarks and brands and distribution venues.

identification The requirement that the licensee place its own name on the product in an inconspicuous manner.

independent contractor Defining the relationship between licensor and licensee in a way stressing that the two are separate entities.

infringement of trademarks Theft of trademark by unauthorized user is covered in this section. Instructions here given by licensor to the licensee as to how to proceed if infringement is discovered in the marketplace.

insurance and indemnity   Clear statements of protection to the licensor for actions by the licensee, as well as insurance requirements imposed on the licensee (typically, product liability). Sometimes, the licensee can also be indemnified.

licensing   For contract purposes, simply the granting of the right to use such properties as patents, processes, business formats, trademarks, brands, or copyrights in return for royalties of other forms of compensation.

manufacturer's agreement   If the licensee is the marketer but not the manufacturer, an addendum to the contract must be drawn up, to be signed by any supplier of the licensee who is producing material with the licensor's trademark/brand name (etc.) on it.

quality and approvals   A wide range of production, marketing, image protection, or other restrictions fall under this heading, wherein the licensor makes known exactly what is required for its name to be associated with the product.

right in trademark   A statement of ownership by the licensor and a declaration of agreed-upon licensee "behavior" while using the trademarks.

royalty   The percentage or unit amount of money charged by the licensor. Also includes up-front advances (if any) and guaranteed minimums (if any).

royalty payment and reporting   Agreed-upon payment procedures, auditing privileges, and bookkeeping requirements.

termination   Probably the contract's most debated part; the specific terms of ending a contract or breaking up an existing relationship.

territory   The geographic range within which the licensee is authorized to produce and/or sell trademarked products.

• **Model makers like Revell, Inc., and promotional licensing, are a perfect fit. The Smithsonian Institution is one licensor to Revell, whose "Smithsonian Collection" includes the Mitsubishi Zero and the ME-262 Schwalbe aircraft.** (Courtesy Revell, Inc.)

trademark notice   Use of proper registration marks to ensure that consumers understand that the trademark does not belong to the licensee but to the licensor.

trademark record   Listing of products and trademarks in the agreement.

The following words and phrases won't be found in licensing contracts, but we use them frequently in the text:

assets/equities   Interchangeable ways of describing (for licensing purposes) intangibles built up by a company—such as consumer goodwill toward the

• **New product development licensing** *par excellance:* **Fisher-Price,** *one of the quality names in toys and trusted by Moms everywhere, applies that "equity" to footwear.*
(Courtesy Little People Footwear, Ltd.)

company or its brands, the reputation of the company itself or its products, strong business relationships that can be capitalized on (for example, having a loyal distributor network).

brand extension/image extension/leveraging   The ability to get the most out of your equity/assets and to multiply the impact of a particular brand beyond its normal market.

image extension   Also applies to the broader benefits enjoyed by the corporation producing a particular brand.

licensee   Independent contractor of licensor; authorized "user" of licensor's property for designated territory, time period, and market.

licensor   Owner of properties: trademark, brand name, patents, processes, logos, business formats, or copyrights.

trademark/brand licensing   What most people in business think of when they hear the word "licensing." The field is so broad, however, as to require segmentation:

   business-to-business or service-to-service licensing   A method of establishing a separate enterprise dedicated to a certain brand or corporate name without actually having to launch a new corporate entity owned and managed by the licensor.

   new product development licensing   A method by which a company generates new product entries into related (but not identical) fields without incurring capital expenditures or inventory risk.

   promotional licensing   A method by which a company extends its advertising exposure without incurring additional cost.

trademark control   Process by which a company safeguards its brand names and trademarks (or other properties). Includes not just conventional infringement protection, but also extending the trademark through licensing that is able to establish trademark use in other, secondary categories.

INDEX